THE BOOK OF

Mexican
FOODS

CHRISTINE BARRETT

Photography by
DAVID RUSSELL

HPBooks

ANOTHER BEST SELLING VOLUME FROM HPBOOKS

HPBooks
Published by The Berkley Publishing Group
200 Madison Avenue
New York, NY 10016

9 8 7

By arrangement with Salamander Books Ltd.

Library of Congress Cataloging-in-Publication Data
Barrett, Christine
   The book of Mexican foods / Christine Barrett.
      p.   cm.
   Includes index.
   ISBN 1-55788-032-8
   1. Cookery, Mexican.   I. Title.
TX716.M4B27   1991
641.5972 – dc20
                                                            91-4770
                                                               CIP

This book was created by Pegasus Editions Limited,
Premier House, Hinton Road, Bournemouth, Dorset BH1 2EF

Printed in Belgium by Proost International Book Production,
Turnhout, Belgium

CONTENTS

INTRODUCTION

Mexico is blessed with an abundance of varied, first-class ingredients, and people who so enjoy food that they make full use of the ingredients to create, with infinite skill, an exciting encyclopedia of colorful dishes. The signatures of Mexican cooking are the crafts of enticing, aromatic smells that herald the rich flavors, fragrant with spices that are blended and trapped inside. However, it is wrong to think that Mexican food is all heavily spiced and hot. Some dishes have subtle flavors to allow the true taste of good-quality produce to shine through, such as Vegetable Soup. When spices are added, they are used with such expertise that the flavors are mellow and harmonious. Not all dishes contain chiles, and those that do can be as hot or mild as you like.

The Book of Mexican Foods shows how to make your own tortillas, and how to transform them into an almost endless variety of dishes, such as quesadillas, empanadas and burritos. There are tantalizing recipes covering the whole range of Mexican eating from free-and-easy tacos and tostadas for today's favorite quick snacks, to dishes suitable for festive occasions, such as Mole Poblano. Also included are mouthwatering vegetable and bean dishes that show that vegetarian food can be fun. Finally, there is a selection of delicious desserts and drinks with the distinctive tastes of Mexico.

One of the joys of Mexican cooking is that it is easy to prepare at home; recipes are not complicated. With few exceptions, ingredients are not difficult to find, and there are no fanciful arrangements, garnishes and decorations. The typical ebullient, friendly and informal Mexican personality is transferred to the food, making it an endless source of relaxed pleasure. The style of cooking we know today as Mexican has evolved over many centuries. It is an amalgam of many influences, fused together over a period of time into a distinct, recognizable style. The foundations lie with the ancient Aztec and Mayan civilizations and the widely disparate foods available to them, such as corn, avocados, fresh and dried beans, sweet potatoes, potatoes, tomatoes, chiles, pumpkins, turkeys, ducks and chocolate, plus a wealth of different fish from the long coastline. From 1519 the conquering Spanish brought with them their favorite produce from the Old World--cattle, for milk and cheese as well as meat; chickens; pigs; rice; wheat; cinnamon; cloves; black pepper; oranges; peaches and apricots.

The Mexicans soon adopted these new foods, but instead of allowing them to change their culinary traditions, they used them to enhance and extend them. In the middle of the nineteenth century, a French dimension was added, as witnessed by many of the delicious breads, cakes and desserts that are still popular. Not surprisingly, as Mexico borders with the United States, nowadays there is a discernible American influence. The U.S. has also helped to popularize Mexican food around the world. Originally there was mostly TexMex food available in the U.S., but now authentic regional Mexican foods are available.

BEANS

Dried beans feature prominently in the Mexican diet. Served in many ways, and incorporated into many dishes, they absorb and blend together spicy flavors, as well as adding nutritional value. Quite a number of different types of dried beans are used, but most of the ones preferred by Mexicans, such as the popular full-flavored, smooth black beans and sweetish, soft-textured pink pinto beans, belong to the kidney bean family. Each gives its special character to a dish, but if a specified type is not available, pinto beans can almost always be substituted.

CHEESE

A crumbly, quite salty white cheese, queso fresco is the most frequently used in Mexico. Good Monterey Jack, farmer cheese or Greek feta are the best substitutes. Queso de Chihuahua is also popular. A mixture of Cheddar and mozzarella cheeses make a good alternative.

CHILES

Chiles are a hallmark of Mexican cooking, being used both raw and cooked to give a distinctive flavor as well as hotness. There are many different varieties of chiles, but only a relatively few are available outside Mexico, and the Southwest. The most commonly found and used varieties are:

Dried ancho chiles are the most commonly used variety in Mexico. They are mild, with a fragrance reminiscent of prunes and raisins, wrinkled and deep reddish-brown, about 5 inches long and 3 inches wide.

Dried mulato chiles are similar in appearance to ancho chiles, but sweeter.

Dried pasilla chiles are long, thin and brownish-black with a fruity piquant flavor.

Jalapeno chiles are a dark rich green and hot, although not as hot as serranos. They are about 2-1/2 inches long and 3/4 inch wide. If unable to buy fresh jalapenos, look for canned ones, but rinse well before using.

Serrano chiles are small, light green, shiny, smooth and very hot. They are also available in cans.

Chiles are not always labelled with their variety, so as a general guide, dried chiles have a more earthy, fruity flavor than fresh ones, smaller chile varieties are invariably hotter than large ones.

Red chiles are not always hotter than green. The seeds and white veins are not only hotter than the flesh, but have less flavor, and are generally removed from the chile before using.

Chiles contain an oil that can make the eyes and even the skin sting, so always avoid touching the eyes after touching chiles. To be really safe, wear rubber gloves when preparing chiles.

In preparing the recipes for this book, unless a variety has been specified, fairly large, quite mild green chiles were used. Other varieties can be substituted according to taste, or what is available. For more flavor and heat, use a hotter variety, or increase the amount.

Further ways to adjust the hotness of cooked dishes are: 1. For flavor without too much heat, use the chile whole and remove before serving. 2. For medium hotness, add several whole chiles and one chile halved lengthwise and seeds discarded. Discard chiles before serving dish. 3. For hot dishes, add chopped or sliced chiles, with or without seeds, remembering that the more seeds you add, the hotter the dish will be.

In Mexico a bowl of pickled jalapeno chiles or a hot relish such as hot chile sauce, is put on the table so people can add extra hotness to their food as they eat.

INGREDIENTS

CHILI POWDER

Chili powder adds an extra flavor dimension to the hotness because in addition to ground dried chiles, it may contain ground cumin and salt and perhaps other seasonings. Chili powder should be added gradually.

HOT PEPPER SAUCE

Hot pepper sauce which is made from a blend of chiles and seasonings, also adds a particular flavor, as well as hotness. There are several brands and each will have its own particular intensity and flavor.

CHAYOTE

Chayote is a type of squash also known as christophene, resembling a ridged-pear with a pale green, fairly thick skin, and crisp white, delicately flavored flesh. Chayotes weigh between 6 to 12 ounces. Although a fruit, they are eaten as a vegetable, sometimes raw in salads, but more often baked, stuffed, added to casseroles or boiled (they can be peeled before or after cooking). The seed of young chayote is edible.

COOKING FAT

Good pork lard is the preferred choice for cooking in Mexico, but because it is not always available, and not to everybody's taste, vegetable oils and butter are usually used in this book. However, good quality lard can be substituted for a true Mexican flavor when frying.

CORN HUSKS

Corn husks are the dried outer leaves of ears of corn and are used to make tamales. They can be bought ready dried but if unavailable a good substitute is to put squares of waxed paper inside squares of foil.

CREAM

Mexican cream is similar to French crème fraîche. which is available in some supermarkets and gourmet stores, or can be made at home by stirring a tablespoonful of natural yogurt into whipping cream and leaving, covered, overnight. Alternatively, use thick sour cream.

MASA HARINA

Masa harina is a type of flour that is made from corn that has been steeped and boiled in lime, dried and very finely ground. It is paler than normal cornmeal and produces heavy doughs. It is used for Corn Tortillas and Tamales. Masa harina is available in most large supermarkets.

TOMATILLOS

Tomatillos belong to the same family as Cape gooseberries, and look like green cherry tomatoes covered in a papery outer casing. They are sometimes referred to as green tomatoes. Their characteristic texture and citrus tang lend body and freshness to dishes. They are usually cooked to develop their lemon-herb flavor and soften their flesh, but occasionally are eaten raw when their sharpness is beneficial, such as in Salsa Verde.

Search for canned tomatillos in specialty food shops if fresh are unavailable. Unripe green ordinary tomatoes are not a good substitute.

TOMATOES

Mexican tomatoes are large and irregularly shaped, similar to beef steak or Mediterranean tomatoes. For the most authentic Mexican flavor, use sun-ripened tomatoes rather than greenhouse-grown ones. If unavailable canned, peeled plum tomatoes can be substituted when making sauces, the most popular way of using tomatoes in Mexico.

TORTILLAS

Tortillas are eaten with meals in the same way as bread, as well as being an integral part of many other dishes.

Corn Tortillas are the traditional version, but in the north of Mexico, near the American border, Wheat Tortillas are now made. They are more difficult to make and quickly become brittle if overcooked, and, so, difficult to fold. They are also more filling.

Tortillas that have been prepared in advance, and are therefore cold, are heated before using, usually in hot oil or on a hot griddle or in a skillet, to make them pliable. A microwave oven can also be used.

There are no hard and fast rules governing the choice of fillings and toppings. They can be varied, mixed and matched to taste. For example, Refried Beans, Picadillo or shredded chicken, turkey or ham, bound with cream cheese, or topped with Salsa Fresca or Salsa Verde or Guacamole. Or perhaps sliced chorizo (spicy Spanish sausage) or diced cheese mixed with cream cheese.

Burritos – are soft, filled and rolled tortillas. See recipe, page 50.

Enchiladas – are filled, rolled tortillas, covered with a sauce and baked. See recipes, pages 40, 42, 46, 65, 93.

Nachos – are fried tortilla chips topped with cheese and chiles, then broiled until the cheese melts. See recipe, page 33.

Quesadillas – are really like tortilla sandwiches which are sold by street vendors and eaten in the open air. They are often filled with green chiles and cheese and then heated. See recipe, page 43.

Tacos – are soft or crisp tortillas that are filled with a sauce and meat mixture, then folded or rolled. These are eaten from your hand. See recipe, page 84.

Tortilla Chips – or totopos are tortillas cut in about eight wedges, then fried until crisp. Tortilla chips are frequently served with dips, such as Guacamole and Bean Dip.

Tostadas – are fried flat tortillas that are topped with beans or meat, lettuce and cheese.

SPECIAL EQUIPMENT

There are only two pieces of special equipment required for Mexican cooking.

Blender or Food Processor — is invaluable for eliminating the large amount of pounding using a pestle and mortar that takes place in a traditional Mexican kitchen.

Tortilla Press — is the best way to ensure sufficiently thin, homemade corn tortillas, which is not easy by hand. Tortilla presses are available from specialty kitchenware shops. To use a tortilla press, line the bottom plate of the press with a square of waxed paper or plastic wrap. Flatten a piece of dough to a thick circle about the size of a small egg, place on the paper, and cover with another piece of waxed paper.

Close the press, pressing the handle down firmly. Open the press, remove the top sheet of paper, then, using the bottom sheet, lift off the tortilla and invert onto a hot griddle or into a skillet. Repeat with remaining dough.

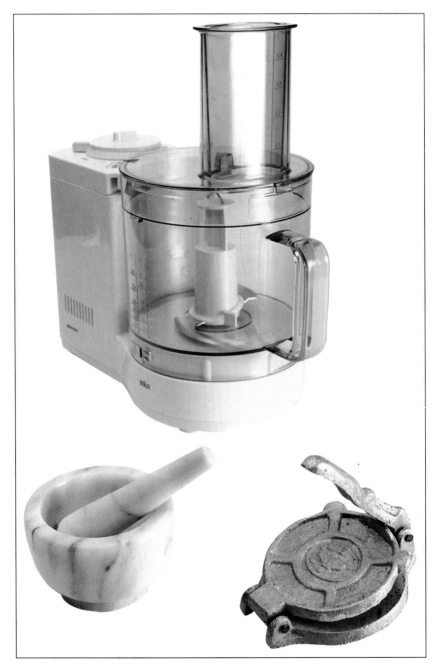

CORN TORTILLAS

2-1/2 cups masa harina
1 teaspoon salt
About 1-1/4 cups warm water

In a large bowl, mix together masa harina and salt. Gradually stir in enough warm water to make a soft but not sticky dough. Divide dough in 12 pieces. To shape by hand, form one piece of dough into a ball, flatten slightly, then put onto a piece of waxed paper. Put a second piece of waxed paper over the top and roll out to a thin circle. Stack between the sheets of waxed paper.

To shape using a tortilla press, see page 12. Heat a griddle or heavy skillet over medium heat until a few drops of cold water will sizzle when sprinkled on it. Carefully peel off the bottom sheet of waxed paper and place tortilla gently on griddle or in skillet. Cook 1 minute or until edges begin to curl, then remove top piece of waxed paper and, using a spatula, turn over tortilla. Cook 1 minute. The first side to be cooked is the top and should be slightly puffy and speckled brown. Stack tortillas on a wire rack, covered with a cloth towel.

Cover with another cloth towel. The tortillas are now ready to eat, fry, refrigerate or freeze.

Makes 12 (6-inch) tortillas.

Note: Corn tortillas can be kept in a sealed plastic bag in the refrigerator up to 5 days, or frozen in a sealed plastic bag 3 months.

— WHOLE-WHEAT TORTILLAS —

2-2/3 cups whole-wheat flour
1 teaspoon salt
3 tablespoons lard or vegetable shortening, diced
1-1/4 cups hot water

Put flour and salt into a large bowl. Cut in the fat with two knives or a pastry blender until mixture resembles bread crumbs. Stir in hot water to form a soft, pliable dough. On a floured board, knead dough until smooth, then cover with a warm, damp cloth towel; let rest 10 minutes.

Divide dough in 12 pieces. Shape one piece in a ball, then flatten. Place on a floured board. Using a floured rolling pin, roll out to a very thin circle (so the board can be seen through the dough). Trim edges if necessary. Stack on a floured plate, making sure there is enough flour on each one to prevent sticking. Heat a griddle or heavy skillet until a few drops of water sizzle when sprinkled on it, then reduce heat slightly. Carefully put a tortilla on the griddle or into skillet.

Cook 30 seconds or until beginning to bubble, turn and cook 10 seconds more. It will look pale and undercooked, if cooked longer, it will become dry and brittle. Stack tortillas on a wire rack covered with a cloth towel, and cover with another cloth towel.

Makes 12 (6-inch) tortillas.

Note: To store, cool, still covered, place a square of waxed paper between each to prevent sticking, store in a sealed plastic bag, in the refrigerator 2 or 3 days.

BASIC BEANS

1 pound pinto beans, soaked overnight
2 tablespoons vegetable oil or beef dripping
1 small onion, chopped
Salt

Drain beans and rinse. Put into a large saucepan, cover with cold water and bring to a boil. Boil 10 minutes. Reduce heat, partly cover the pan with the lid and simmer 3 hours or until the beans are very soft. Add more boiling water, if necessary.

Heat oil, add onion and cook until golden. Add to beans, season with salt and simmer 5 minutes or until the bean liquid thickens. Use immediately or cool quickly and store in a covered container in the refrigerator up to 2 days.

Makes 8 servings.

REFRIED BEANS

2 tablespoons olive oil
1/2 recipe Basic Beans, page 15
2 ounces queso fresca or Monterey Jack cheese,
    shredded (1/2 cup)

Heat oil in a skillet over medium heat. Add beans and mash together with a fork or wooden spoon to make a thick paste. If mixture sticks, add another tablespoon of oil or some water.

Serve sprinkled with shredded cheese. Refried beans can also be served without the cheese.

Makes 4 servings.

—COOKED TOMATO SAUCE—

1 tablespoon olive oil
1 small onion, finely chopped
1 garlic clove, finely chopped
1 pound tomatoes, peeled, chopped
1 green chile
1 tablespoon tomato paste
1 teaspoon finely chopped cilantro
Salt and pepper

Heat oil in a skillet, add onion and garlic and cook 5 minutes until soft but not
brown. Add tomatoes, chile, tomato paste
and cilantro; season with salt and pepper.

Simmer 20 minutes or until thick.
Remove the chile. For a hotter sauce,
chop the chile and return to sauce.

Makes 2 cups.

PICADILLO

8 ounces ground beef
8 ounces lean ground pork
2 tablespoons red wine vinegar
Salt and pepper
1 tablespoon olive oil
1 small onion, finely chopped
1 garlic clove, finely chopped
1 green chile, finely chopped
1 pound tomatoes, peeled, chopped
1/3 cup raisins
1/2 cup slivered almonds
1/2 teaspoon ground cloves
1 teaspoon ground cinnamon
2 tablespoons tomato paste

Mix meats together with vinegar, salt and pepper. Heat oil in a large skillet, add onion, garlic and chile and cook 3 minutes, stirring frequently. Add meat mixture and stir over high heat until beginning to brown. Drain off fat.

Stir in tomatoes, raisins, almonds, cloves, cinnamon and tomato paste. Simmer 15 minutes, uncovered, or until mixture is thick and well blended. Use hot as a filling for tortillas, enchiladas, chimichangas, burritos or tacos, or use cold as a filling for empanadas.

Makes 4 to 6 servings.

VERMICELLI SOUP

2 tablespoons olive oil
2 ounces vermicelli, broken
1 medium-size onion, chopped
1 garlic clove, finely chopped
1 pound tomatoes, peeled, seeded and chopped
8 cups beef stock
Salt and pepper
1/4 cup dry sherry
1 tablespoon finely chopped cilantro, to garnish
Grated Parmesan cheese, to serve

Heat oil in a skillet over medium-low heat. Add vermicelli and sauté until golden. Drain vermicelli and set aside; reserving oil. Place onion, garlic and tomatoes in a blender or food processor fitted with the metal blade; process until pureed. Heat reserved oil in skillet over medium heat, then pour in tomato mixture. Cook 5 minutes, stirring constantly.

Put vermicelli, tomato mixture and stock into a large saucepan. Season with salt and pepper. Bring to a boil. Reduce heat, cover and simmer 10 minutes or until vermicelli is tender. Stir in sherry. Pour into a warmed tureen. Garnish with chopped cilantro. Serve with grated Parmesan cheese.

Makes 6 to 8 servings.

— CHICKEN TORTILLA SOUP —

3-3/4 cups chicken stock
1 pasilla chile
2 tablespoons olive oil
4 Corn Tortillas, page 13, cut in 1/2-inch strips
1 small onion, finely chopped
6 ounces cooked chicken, shredded
2 tablespoons fresh lime juice
Salt and pepper

Bring 3/4 cup of the chicken stock to a boil. Add chile and let stand 30 minutes. Drain; reserve stock. Discard stem and seeds of the chile; chop flesh finely. Reserve.

Heat oil in a heavy saucepan over medium heat. Add tortilla strips and fry until golden. Drain on paper towels. Add onion to oil left in pan, adding a little more if necessary. Cook onion over low heat until soft but not brown. Add all the stock and simmer 10 minutes, skimming off any foam that comes to the surface. Add chicken and lime juice and season with salt and pepper; simmer 5 minutes.

Place tortilla strips in a warmed soup tureen or individual bowls, and top with hot soup. Garnish with the reserved chopped chile.

Makes 6 servings.

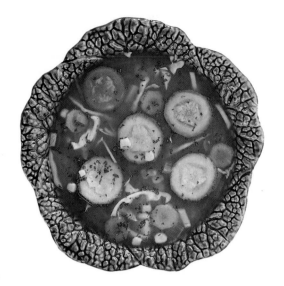

VEGETABLE SOUP

4 cups chicken stock
2 cups water
1 pound tomatoes, peeled and chopped
1 large onion, finely chopped
1 garlic clove, crushed with 1 teaspoon salt
8 whole black peppercorns
4 whole cloves
1 large potato, cubed
1 medium-size zucchini, sliced
1/2 small head cabbage, thinly sliced
2 medium-size carrots, sliced
1/2 cup thinly sliced celery
1/2 cup whole-kernel corn (fresh, cooked or frozen)
Chopped cilantro, to garnish

Place chicken stock, water, tomatoes, onion and garlic in a large saucepan. Tie peppercorns and cloves in a piece of cheesecloth and add to pan. Bring to a boil. Reduce heat, cover and simmer 40 minutes. Add potato, zucchini, cabbage, carrots, celery and corn. Cover and simmer about 10 minutes or until all the vegetables are tender. Discard cheesecloth bag.

Pour soup into a warmed tureen and garnish with chopped cilantro.

Makes 6 to 8 servings.

——— AVOCADO SOUP ———

2 large avocados
1 cup whipping cream
4 cups chicken stock
3 tablespoons dry sherry
Salt
2 tablespoons chopped cilantro, to garnish

Cut avocados in half lengthwise, remove seeds and scoop flesh into a blender or food processor fitted with the metal blade. Add half of the cream and process until smooth. Add half of the remaining cream and process again until just combined. Place chicken stock in a medium-size saucepan and bring to a boil.

Remove from heat and gradually whisk in avocado puree. Add sherry. Heat gently, but do not boil. Season with salt. Remove from heat. Pour into a warmed soup tureen. Serve hot or cold with the remaining cream swirled over the top and sprinkled with chopped cilantro.

Makes 4 to 6 servings.

BEAN SOUP

6 ounces dried red kidney beans, soaked overnight
5 cups water
1 medium-size onion, chopped
1 garlic clove, crushed
1-1/2 teaspoons chili powder
Salt
2 ounces mozzarella cheese, shredded (1/2 cup)
4 ounces croutons, to garnish

Drain beans and rinse well under cold running water. In a large saucepan bring the water to a boil. Add beans. Bring to a boil; boil 10 minutes. Reduce heat, cover and simmer 2 hours or until beans are tender.

Add onion, garlic and chili powder; simmer 30 to 40 minutes. Place, in batches, in a blender or food processor fitted with the metal blade; process until smooth. Add more water if necessary. Return soup to saucepan and reheat. Season with salt.

Serve in a warmed soup tureen, sprinkled with cheese and garnished with croutons.

Makes 4 servings.

CORN SOUP

2 tablespoons butter
1 small onion, finely chopped
1 garlic clove crushed in 1 teaspoon salt
3 small tomatoes, peeled and chopped
5 cups chicken stock
1 bay leaf
8 to 10 ounces whole-kernel corn (fresh, canned
    or frozen)
Salt
2/3 cup half and half
2 tablespoons chopped cilantro, to garnish

In a large saucepan, melt butter over low heat. Add onion and garlic; cook until onion is soft but not brown. Add tomatoes. Simmer 10 minutes. Add stock, bay leaf and corn. Season with salt to taste. Bring to a boil. Reduce heat, cover and simmer 30 minutes. Discard bay leaf. Pour soup, in batches, into a blender or food processor fitted with the metal blade and process until pureed.

Return soup to saucepan. Stir in half and half and heat to just below the boiling point; do not boil. Serve in a warmed tureen, sprinkled with chopped cilantro.

Makes 6 servings.

—SHRIMP WITH CHILE CHEESE—

1/2 recipe Cooked Tomato Sauce, page 17
2/3 cup dairy sour cream
Few drops hot pepper sauce
2 ounces Cheddar cheese, shredded (1/2 cup)
1 green chile, finely chopped
Salt
24 large cooked shrimp in their shells
Lemon wedges, to garnish

In a bowl, combine all the ingredients except shrimp and lemon wedges together in a bowl. Adjust seasonings to taste.

Serve dip in individual dishes on a plate with shrimp around the outside, tails facing out. Garnish with lemon wedges.

Makes 6 servings.

Note: The dip may also be served with tortilla chips.

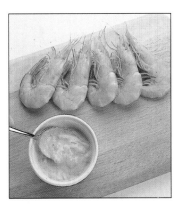

GUACAMOLE

1/2 small onion, finely chopped
4 tomatoes, peeled, seeded and finely chopped
1 green chile, seeded and finely chopped
1/2 small green bell pepper, seeded and finely
    chopped
1 tablespoon chopped cilantro
2 large ripe avocados
Salt and black pepper
2 teaspoons lemon juice
tortilla chips, page 10, or raw vegetables, to serve

In a bowl, mix together onion, tomatoes, chile, bell pepper and cilantro. Cut avocados in half lengthwise, remove seed and scoop out flesh.

Mash roughly with tomato mixture. Season with salt and black pepper, and stir in lemon juice. Transfer to a serving bowl. Serve immediately with Tortilla Chips or vegetables.

Makes 6 servings.

— MARINATED MUSHROOMS —

2 tablespoons olive oil
1 garlic clove
8 ounces mushrooms, thickly sliced
1 medium-size onion, thinly sliced
1 carrot, finely grated
1 celery stalk, thinly sliced
1 green bell pepper, thinly sliced
1 green chile, seeded, finely chopped
Juice of 2 lemons
1 tablespoon chopped cilantro
Salt and black pepper

Heat oil in a heavy skillet, add garlic and cook until golden. Discard garlic. To the skillet, add mushrooms, onion, carrot, celery, bell pepper and chile. Cook over low heat 5 minutes. Add lemon juice and cilantro; season with salt and black pepper.

Cover and simmer 5 minutes. Cool completely, then transfer to a serving bowl.

Makes 4 servings .

BEAN DIP

1/4 cup butter
1 small onion, chopped
1 garlic clove, chopped
1 teaspoon ground cinnamon
1 teaspoon chili powder
1/2 teaspoon ground cumin
1/2 recipe Basic Beans, page 15
2 ounces sharp Cheddar cheese, shredded
  (1/2 cup)
Salt
Hot pepper sauce (optional)
Tortilla Chips, page 11, to serve

In a saucepan, melt butter over low heat ; add onion, garlic, cinnamon, chili powder and cumin. Cook 10 minutes or until onion has softened. Add Basic Beans and cheese and stir until melted.

Spoon mixture into a blender or food processor fitted with the metal blade; process until smooth, in batches if necessary. Season with salt and hot pepper sauce, if desired. If mixture is too thick, add water 1 tablespoon at a time . Spoon into a serving dish. Serve with Tortilla Chips.

Makes 6 to 8 servings.

CEVICHE

1 pound firm white fish fillets, such as haddock,
  cod or bass
1/3 cup fresh lime juice
2/3 cup olive oil
2 green onions, finely chopped
1 garlic clove, finely chopped
2 tablespoons finely chopped cilantro
Few drops of hot pepper sauce
Salt

Rinse fish, dry and cut in thin strips across
the grain. Place in a non-metallic bowl. Pour
lime juice over fish, cover and marinate
1 hour, but preferably overnight in the
refrigerator — the fish will become opaque.
In a serving bowl, combine olive oil, onions,
garlic, half the cilantro and hot pepper
sauce. Season with salt.

Drain fish and add to serving bowl. Toss
gently, making sure fish is well coated.
Sprinkle with remaining cilantro .

Makes 6 servings .

Variation: Use 12 ounces of scallops instead of white fish; slice each horizontally in
two or three even slices.

- STUFFED VEGETABLE KEBABS -

4 small zucchini
4 ounces button mushrooms
4 ounces cherry tomatoes
8 ounces ground lamb or beef
1 small onion, finely chopped
1 tablespoon finely chopped cilantro
1/4 teaspoon ground cumin
Large pinch red (cayenne) pepper
1 egg, beaten
Salt and pepper
Olive oil for brushing on vegetables

Cut zucchini in l-inch chunks, then steam 5 minutes. Drain. Using a teaspoon, scoop out center 1/2 inch from one end. Remove mushroom stalks, finely chop and reserve. Slice off tops of tomatoes; using a teaspoon, carefully scoop out seeds. In a medium-size bowl, combine meat, onion, cilantro, cumin, cayenne, egg and mushroom stalks. Season with salt and pepper.

Preheat broiler.

Stuff zucchini, tomatoes and mushroom caps with meat mixture, and thread alternately on to skewers so they are touching closely. Brush with olive oil and broil 10 minutes on each side, making sure they do not burn.

Makes 6 servings.

Note: Any leftover filling mixture can be cooked and served with Tortilla Chips, page 11.

STUFFED EGGS

1 medium-size avocado
· 6 hard-cooked eggs, halved lengthwise
1 small onion, very finely chopped
1 small green bell pepper, very finely chopped
4 ounces cooked shrimp, shelled, deveined and
    chopped
1 teaspoon lemon juice
1 teaspoon white wine vinegar
Salt and black pepper
Large pinch red (cayenne) pepper
Shredded lettuce, to serve
1 tomato, sliced, to serve
1 tablespoon finely chopped cilantro, to garnish

Cut avocado in half lengthwise, remove seed and scoop flesh into a blender or food processor fitted with the metal blade. Using a teaspoon, scoop out egg yolks into the blender or food processor; blend until smooth.

Transfer to a medium-size bowl. Stir in onion, bell pepper, shrimp, lemon juice, vinegar, salt, black pepper and cayenne. Using a teaspoon, place generous amounts of the mixture into egg whites. Arrange on a bed of shredded lettuce and tomato slices. Sprinkle with cilantro.

Makes 6 servings.

– STUFFED ROAST BEEF ROLLS –

1 medium-size avocado
1 small zucchini, peeled, sliced and steamed
1/2 cup very finely chopped onion
1/2 teaspoon chili powder
2 tablespoons olive oil
2 tablespoons white wine vinegar
Salt
16 thin slices cold roast beef
Lettuce leaves
3 hard-cooked eggs
Radishes, to garnish

Cut avocado in half lengthwise, discard seed and scoop flesh into a blender or food processor fitted with the metal blade. Add zucchini and process until smooth. Transfer to a medium-size bowl. Stir in onion, chili powder, oil and vinegar. Mix well and season with salt. Place a tablespoon of the mixture on each slice of beef, roll up and secure with a wooden pick. Reserve any remaining avocado mixture.

Place lettuce leaves on a flat plate. Arrange beef rolls in a circle, like spokes of a wheel. Halve eggs lengthwise. Scoop out and sieve yolks. Place in center of serving dish. Cut egg whites into thin strips and place on roast beef rolls. Garnish with radishes. Serve any reserved avocado mixture separately.

Makes 8 servings.

NACHOS

Vegetable oil, for frying
6 Corn Tortillas, page 13

Topping:
3 ounces Cheddar cheese, shredded (3/4 cup)
1 medium-size onion, finely chopped
1 green bell pepper, finely chopped
1 green chile, finely chopped
1 pickled jalapeno chile, finely chopped, if desired
1 teaspoon chili powder
2/3 cup dairy sour cream

Pour oil into a large heavy skillet to 1 inch deep. Heat oil, and when it is hot, lower a tortilla into oil using tongs. When tortilla turns golden brown and is crisp, remove quickly and drain on paper towels. Keep warm. Repeat with remaining tortillas.

Preheat broiler.

Break each tortilla in 8 pieces and lay in a single layer on bottom of a broiler pan. Put a layer of shredded cheese on each piece of tortilla, then a layer of onion, then bell pepper, then the chiles. Sprinkle with chili powder and spoon a little sour cream over the top. Broil until sour cream is bubbling and cheese has melted, moving farther from heat if necessary.

Makes 6 servings.

SAVORY TAMALES

30 dried corn husks, soaked overnight in cold
    water (see Note)

Filling:
1 pound green tomatillos, peeled
12 cilantro sprigs
Salt and pepper
1 tablespoon olive oil
1/2 onion, chopped
12 ounces cooked chicken, shredded

Dough:
3 cups masa harina
Salt
1-1/2 cups warm water
1/2 cup lard, softened
1-1/4 cups warm beef stock
2 teaspoons baking powder

To make filling, put tomatillos into a
saucepan, barely cover with water and
bring to a boil. Reduce heat and simmer 5
minutes. Drain; reserve liquid.

In a blender or food processor fitted
with the metal blade; process tomatillos,
cilantro, salt, pepper and enough of the
reserved liquid to make a fairly thick
paste. Heat oil in a heavy skillet, add
onion and cook 2 or 3 minutes. Stir in
tomatillo paste and simmer about 20
minutes, adding more liquid if necessary
to maintain a fairly thick paste. Set aside.

To make dough, in a bowl mix together masa harina, salt, water and lard. Slowly stir in stock. Add baking powder and beat with a wooden spoon until bubbles appear and a teaspoonful dropped in a glass of cold water floats and sticks together. Drain and pat dry corn husks. Place 2 husks overlapping in palm of one hand and spoon on 1 tablespoon of sauce, 1 tablespoon dough, a little cooked chicken and another spoonful of sauce.

Wrap husks carefully to enclose filling, then fold tail towards top, leaving it loose to allow room for expansion.   Place tamales in the top half of a steamer and cover with waxed paper. Cover tightly and steam 1-1/2 hours until dough is light and fluffy. Reheat any remaining sauce and serve separately.

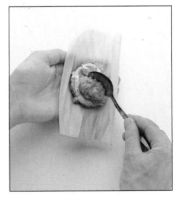

Variations: Substitute Cooked Tomato Sauce, for tomatillo sauce. Use   pork, beef, fish or turkey instead of chicken.

Note: If dried corn husks are not available, use 30 (8-inch) squares of foil covered with squares of waxed paper. Place sauce, dough, chicken, then more sauce in center. Fold foil over loosely, sealing edges to make them watertight.

Makes 6 servings.

CORN SOUFFLE

1/4 cup butter
1/2 medium-size onion, finely chopped
1 (8-oz.) can whole-kernel corn, drained
3 eggs, separated
2 green chiles, seeded and chopped
Salt

Preheat oven to 375F (19OC). Grease an 8-inch soufflé dish, and sprinkle the inside lightly with flour.

In a medium-size saucepan, melt butter. Add onion and cook until soft but not brown. Transfer to a blender or food processor fitted with the metal blade. Add corn and egg yolks. Process until as smooth as possible. Transfer to a large bowl. Stir in chiles and salt.

In a medium-size bowl, whisk egg whites until stiff but not dry. Gently fold into corn mixture just until combined. Transfer mixture to soufflé dish. Bake 10 minutes; reduce temperature to 350F (175C) and bake 20 to 30 minutes or until lightly brown, and just set in center. Serve immediately.

Makes 4 servings.

—— EGGS VALLEJO STYLE ——

2 tablespoons butter
1 small onion, thinly sliced
1 green chile, seeded, cut in strips
1 pound tomatoes, peeled, seeded and chopped
2 tablespoons tomato paste
Salt and pepper
6 eggs
3 ounces Cheddar cheese, shredded (3/4 cup)

Melt butter in a large, heavy skillet. Add onion and cook over medium heat until soft but not brown. Stir in chile, tomatoes and tomato paste. Simmer 10 minutes.

Season with salt and pepper. Make four indentations in mixture. Break eggs one at a time onto a saucer, then carefully slide into indentations, cover and simmer about 4 minutes until egg whites are set.

Top each egg with cheese, cover and cook 1 minute until cheese has melted. Serve immediately.

Makes 6 servings.

——— RANCH-STYLE EGGS ———

1 recipe Cooked Tomato Sauce, page 17
1/2 recipe Refried Beans, page 16
Vegetable oil, for frying
8 Corn Tortillas, page 13
8 eggs
2 thin slices cooked ham, diced
1/2 (l0-oz.) package frozen green peas, cooked
1 banana, to garnish

In separate saucepans, gently heat Tomato Sauce and Refried Beans. Keep hot.

Pour oil into a heavy skillet over medium heat to 1/4 inch deep. Fry each tortilla until crisp and brown. Drain on paper towels. Keep tortillas warm. Fry eggs in same oil. Divide half of the Tomato Sauce between four warmed plates.

Place a spoonful of Refried Beans on sauce, then top with a tortilla. Place 2 eggs side by side on tortilla and cover with a second tortilla. Spoon over the remaining Tomato Sauce. Sprinkle with ham and peas. Peel and slice banana, then use to garnish.

Makes 4 servings.

EGGS WITH POTATOES & HAM

2 large or 4 medium-size baking potatoes, peeled
2 tablespoons olive oil
1 small onion, finely chopped
4 ounces cooked lean ham, chopped
4 eggs
1 avocado, to garnish
Cilantro sprigs, to garnish

Cut potatoes in 1/4-inch-thick slices, then in 1/4-inch dice. Rinse with cold water. Drain well and pat dry on paper towels.

Heat oil in a heavy skillet. Add potatoes and onion, cover and cook over medium heat, stirring frequently, or until tender, about 15 minutes. Add ham, mix well and heat 5 minutes.

With back of a large spoon, make four indentations in mixture. Break eggs, one at a time onto a saucer, then carefully slide into each indentation. Cover, and cook until eggs are set, about 5 minutes. Peel, seed and slice avocado. Serve eggs and potatoes garnished with avocado slices and cilantro.

Makes 4 servings.

— EGG-FILLED ENCHILADAS —

1/3 cup vegetable oil
8 Whole-Wheat Tortillas, page 14
1 recipe Cooked Tomato Sauce, page 17
4 hard-cooked eggs
2/3 cup dairy sour cream
Salt and pepper
2 tablespoons chopped cilantro, to garnish

Preheat oven to 375F (19OC). Grease a shallow ovenproof dish.

Heat oil in a heavy skillet over medium heat. Using tongs, carefully place one tortilla at a time in hot oil, hold in oil 3 to 5 seconds until soft, then turn over and repeat on second side. Drain on paper towels and keep warm.

Meanwhile, in a saucepan over low heat, warm Cooked Tomato Sauce, stirring occasionally. Mash eggs and sour cream in a bowl; season with salt and pepper. Spoon onto tortillas and roll up. Place seam-side down in ovenproof dish. Spoon Tomato Sauce over rolled tortillas. Cover with foil and bake 15 to 20 minutes until heated through. Garnish with cilantro and serve immediately.

Makes 4 servings.

CHIMICHANGAS

12 (6-inch) Whole-Wheat Tortillas, page 14
Vegetable oil, for deep-frying
Guacamole, page 26

Filling:
1 tablespoon olive oil
1 small onion, finely chopped
1 garlic clove, finely chopped
1 green chile, seeded and finely chopped
1 jalapeno chile, finely chopped
1/2 green bell pepper, finely chopped
2 medium-size potatoes, diced and cooked
2/3 cup dairy sour cream
8 ounces Cheddar cheese, shredded (2 cups)

To prepare filling, heat oil in a small skillet. Add onion, garlic, chiles and bell pepper. Cook over medium heat until soft but not brown. Add potato and mix well. Set aside. Heat a heavy skillet until drops of water will sizzle when sprinkled on it. Place a tortilla in skillet to warm 30 seconds. Repeat on other side. Place a spoonful of onion mixture in center, top with a spoonful of sour cream, then some Cheddar cheese. Fold in ends, then roll and secure with a wooden pick. Repeat with remaining tortillas and filling. Refrigerate 30 minutes.

Heat oil in a deep skillet or pan over medium heat. Fry chimichangas a few at a time about 5 minutes or until golden brown. Drain on paper towels; keep warm. Or, shallow fry 3 minutes on each side and drain. Discard wooden picks and serve hot with Guacamole.

Makes 6 servings.

- CHEESE-FILLED ENCHILADAS -

3 tablespoons vegetable oil
12 Whole-Wheat Tortillas, page 14, or Corn
  Tortillas, page 13
1 recipe Cooked Tomato Sauce, page 17
1 teaspoon hot chili powder
1 ounce Parmesan cheese, grated (1/3 cup)
1 tablespoon chopped cilantro

Filling:
1-1/2 pounds cottage cheese
12 ounces queso fresco or Monterey Jack cheese,
  shredded (3 cups)
1-1/2 teaspoons mustard powder
2 garlic cloves, finely chopped
Pepper

Heat oven to 375F (19OC). Grease a large, shallow ovenproof dish.

To make filling, mix all ingredients in a bowl; set aside. Heat oil in a heavy skillet. Using tongs, carefully place one tortilla at a time in hot oil. Cook 3 to 5 seconds or until softened. Quickly turn over tortilla and repeat on second side. Drain on paper towels; keep warm. Repeat with all tortillas.

Divide filling between warm tortillas, roll up and pack together, seam-side down, in dish. Stir chili powder into Cooked Tomato Sauce, pour over enchiladas and sprinkle with Parmesan cheese. Cover with foil and bake 45 minutes. Remove foil and bake 15 minutes to brown. Remove from oven, sprinkle with cilantro and serve hot.

Makes 6 servings.

QUESADILLAS

12 Corn Tortillas, page 13
About 3/4 cup dairy sour cream
6 ounces Cheddar cheese, shredded (1-1/2 cups)
1 small onion, very finely chopped
1 teaspoon chili powder
1 green chile, finely chopped
1 tablespoon finely chopped cilantro
Guacamole, page 26

Separately heat each tortilla in a hot dry skillet 30 seconds. Place a tablespoon of sour cream on one half of a tortilla, top with cheese, then onion. Sprinkle with chili powder, chile and cilantro. Fold over the other half of the tortilla and secure with a wooden pick. Repeat with remaining tortillas.

Heat a skillet until a few drops of water sizzle when sprinkled on it. Place one in skillet at a time. Cook on one side 45 seconds. Turn. Repeat until cheese melts. Serve immediately as an appetizer with Guacamole or as a snack.

Makes 6 servings .

Note: Quesadillas may be placed on a baking sheet, covered with foil, baked on top shelf of a preheated 375F (19OC) oven 15 minutes.

TORTILLAS WITH CREAM & CHEESE

1/3 cup vegetable oil
1 medium-size onion, finely chopped
1 garlic clove, finely chopped
1 pound tomatoes, peeled, seeded and pureed
1 teaspoon finely chopped cilantro
Salt and pepper
12 Whole-Wheat Tortillas, page 14, cut in
    l-inch-wide strips
1 cup whipping cream
3 ounces Parmesan cheese, grated (1 cup)

Preheat oven to 375F (190C). Grease a l-quart ovenproof dish.

Heat 2 tablespoons of the oil in a saucepan over medium heat. Add onion and garlic; cook until soft but not brown. Add tomatoes and cilantro; season with salt and pepper. Simmer about 10 minutes or until reduced in volume.

Heat remaining oil in a skillet over medium heat and fry tortilla strips 45 seconds on each side, without browning. Drain on paper towels. Pour half the tomato sauce into dish. Top with tortilla strips, then cream, and top with remaining sauce. Sprinkle with Parmesan cheese. Bake 20 minutes.

Makes 6 servings.

- TUNA & CHEESE CASSEROLE -

1 tablespoon olive oil
1 medium-size onion, chopped
1 garlic clove, crushed in 1/2 teaspoon salt
1 pound tomatoes, peeled and chopped
1 tablespoon tomato paste
8 ripe pitted olives, sliced
1 green chile, seeded and chopped
1/2 green bell pepper, chopped
1 teaspoon ground cumin
1 (6-1/2-oz.) can tuna, drained, flaked
3/4 cup cottage cheese
1 egg
6 ounces Cheddar cheese, shredded (1-1/2 cups)
4 Corn Tortillas, page 13, or Whole-Wheat
    Tortillas, page 14, cut in strips

Preheat oven to 350F (175C).

Heat oil in a medium-size saucepan, add onion and garlic and cook until soft but not brown. Add tomatoes, tomato paste, olives, chile, bell pepper and cumin. Bring to a boil. Reduce heat, cover and simmer 15 minutes or until fairly thick; remove lid if necessary. Stir in tuna.

Mix cottage cheese with egg. Place half the tomato mixture in a shallow ovenproof dish. Cover with half the Cheddar cheese. Spread cottage cheese mixture over top, then cover with tortilla strips. Spoon the remaining tomato mixture over tortilla strips. Sprinkle with the remaining Cheddar cheese. Bake 30 minutes or until bubbling and golden brown.

Makes 4 servings.

—— CRAB ENCHILADAS ——

3 tablespoons vegetable oil
12 Whole-Wheat Tortillas, page 14, or Corn
    Tortillas, page 13
1 recipe Cooked Tomato Sauce, page 17
2/3 cup dairy sour cream
1 tablespoon chopped cilantro, to garnish
2 tablespoons toasted slivered almonds, to garnish

Filling:
1 tablespoon olive oil
1 small onion, finely chopped
1 small garlic clove, finely chopped
6 ounces cooked crab, flaked
3 pitted green olives, chopped
1/4 cup raisins
1/4 cup chopped almonds
1 tablespoon chopped cilantro
1 teaspoon capers
Salt

Preheat oven to 350F (175C). Grease a shallow ovenproof dish. To make filling, heat olive oil in a medium-size saucepan. Add onion and garlic. Cook until soft but not brown, 5 to 10 minutes. Stir in crab, olives and raisins. Heat 3 to 5 minutes. Keep warm.

To make enchiladas, heat vegetable oil in a large heavy skillet. Using tongs, carefully place one tortilla at a time in hot oil. Hold 3 to 5 seconds until softened. Quickly turn tortilla and repeat on second side. Drain on paper towels.

In a saucepan over low heat, warm Cooked Tomato Sauce, stirring occasionally. Spoon filling onto each tortilla, roll up, and place, seam-side down, in ovenproof dish.

Pour tomato sauce over the enchiladas, cover with foil and bake 15 minutes to heat through. Remove foil; top enchiladas with sour cream.

Return to oven 5 to 10 minutes to warm sour cream. Sprinkle with cilantro and toasted almonds.

Makes 6 servings.

— BAKED SPICED FISH —

1/4 green bell pepper, chopped
1/4 red bell pepper, chopped
2 tablespoons finely chopped cilantro leaves
1 teaspoon ground cumin
1/2 teaspoon chili powder
1 garlic clove, crushed
Salt
1 tablespoon white wine vinegar
1 (2-1b.) whole sea bream or other fish, ready to
   cook
2 tablespoons butter
About 1-1/4 cups milk
3 tablespoons cornstarch

Preheat oven to 350F (175C).

In a medium-size bowl, mix together bell peppers, cilantro, cumin, chili powder, garlic, salt and vinegar. Place fish on a large sheet of foil that will enclose it completely; place on a baking sheet. Stuff fish with pepper mixture, spreading any remaining mixture over top. Dot with butter. Fold foil over fish and seal edges tightly. Bake 25 minutes or until fish turns from translucent to opaque. Carefully unwrap fish and transfer to a warmed serving plate; reserve baking juices. Cover fish and keep warm.

Strain baking juices into a measuring cup. Add enough milk to make 1-3/4 cups. In a medium-size saucepan, mix cornstarch with a little of the liquid to make a paste, then gradually stir in remaining liquid. Bring to a boil, stirring constantly with a wooden spoon. Reduce heat and simmer 1 minute. Adjust seasoning if necessary. Pour into a warmed sauce boat and serve with fish.

Makes 6 servings.

——— FISH IN GREEN SAUCE ———

1 pound tomatillos or green tomatoes
3 green onions, chopped
1 tablespoon chopped cilantro
1 garlic clove, chopped
1 small green chile, chopped
2 teaspoons olive oil
Salt
1 pound haddock fillets or other white fish fillets
3 tablespoons fresh lime juice
3 tablespoons vegetable oil

Remove paper husks from tomatillos and rinse. If using green tomatoes, peel.

Pour cold water into a medium-size saucepan to 1/2 inch deep. Place tomatillos or green tomatoes in pan. Bring to a boil. Reduce heat, cover and simmer 10 minutes or until tender. Drain and cool. Place tomatillos or green tomatoes in a blender or food processor fitted with the metal blade. Add green onions, cilantro, garlic and chile; process until pureed.

Heat olive oil in a pan. Add tomatillo mixture, and season with salt. Bring to a boil, reduce heat and simmer, uncovered, 15 minutes. Keep warm. Sprinkle fish with lime juice, then with salt. Let stand 5 minutes. Heat vegetable oil in a large skillet. Add fish and cook 1 minute on each side. Pour sauce over fish, cover and simmer 5 minutes, or until fish turns from translucent to opaque. Serve hot.

Makes 4 servings.

—— BAKED FISH BURRITOS ——

12 Whole-Wheat Tortillas, page 14
3 ounces Cheddar cheese, shredded (3/4 cup)
Guacamole, page 26, shredded lettuce and
    tomato, to serve

Filling:
12 ounces cod fillets or other firm white fish
1 tablespoon olive oil
1 small onion, finely chopped
1 green chile, finely chopped
1/2 teaspoon chili powder
2/3 cup dairy sour cream
1 tablespoon finely chopped cilantro
Salt and pepper

Preheat oven to 350F (175C). Grease a large shallow ovenproof dish.

To make filling, rinse fish with cold water and pat dry with paper towels. Place fish in a large skillet. Barely cover with water, and season with salt and pepper. Bring to a boil, then reduce heat so liquid barely moves. Cover and poach 5 to 7 minutes or until fish turns from translucent to opaque.

Drain fish; discard liquid. Flake fish, carefully removing any bones and skin. Put fish into a bowl. Heat oil in a small skillet. Add onion, chile and chili powder; cook until soft. Drain off excess oil, and add onion and chile to fish. Add sour cream and cilantro and season with salt and pepper; mix well.

To make burritos, warm each tortilla in a ungreased hot skillet 40 seconds until pliable. Remove from pan.

Fold 2 sides of a tortilla in to center, overlapping edges a little. Fold edge nearest you towards center, forming a pocket; fill pocket with fish mixture. Fold over open edge. Secure with a wooden pick, then place burrito in prepared dish. Repeat until all burritos are filled.

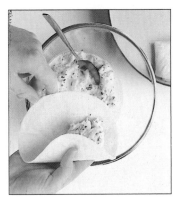

Sprinkle with cheese, cover with foil and bake 20 minutes. Discard wooden picks. Serve with Guacamole, shredded lettuce and tomato.

Makes 6 servings.

RED SNAPPER VERACRUZ STYLE

2 tablespoons olive oil
1 medium-size onion, chopped
3 garlic cloves, very finely chopped
1 pound tomatoes, peeled and chopped
10 pitted green olives, chopped
2 tablespoons capers
3 bay leaves
6 black peppercorns
Salt
2 pounds red snapper fillets or other white fish
    fillets

Heat oil in a large saucepan. Add onion and garlic, and cook 5 to 10 minutes until soft but not brown. Add tomatoes, olives, capers, bay leaves, peppercorns and salt. Bring to a boil, then reduce heat and simmer, uncovered, 10 minutes.

Place fish into a large skillet and sprinkle with salt. Pour tomato mixture over fish. Bring to a boil. Reduce heat, cover and simmer about 7 minutes or until fish turns from translucent to opaque. Discard bay leaves. Serve hot.

Makes 6 servings.

⸺ FISH IN GARLIC SAUCE ⸺

1 pound haddock or sole fillets
Juice of 1 small lime
Salt and pepper
3 tablespoons olive oil
3 garlic cloves, chopped
3 tablespoons vegetable oil
1 tablespoon chopped cilantro

Wipe fish with damp paper towels. Pour lime juice over fish, and sprinkle with salt and pepper. Let stand at least 30 minutes.

Heat olive oil in a small saucepan, over medium heat. Add garlic and cook until light golden brown. Keep warm. Pat fish dry with paper towels. Meanwhile, heat vegetable oil in a large skillet. Add fish fillets and cook until fish turns from translucent to opaque, about 5 to 7 minutes, turning once.

Divide fish among four warmed plates. Spoon garlic and oil over each serving. Sprinkle with cilantro and serve hot.

Makes 4 servings.

─ COD YUCATAN STYLE ─

4 cod fillets (4 to 6 ounces each)
2 tablespoons fresh lime juice
Salt and pepper
1 tablespoon olive oil
1 small onion, finely chopped
1 small green bell pepper, chopped
2 ounces pumpkin seeds
2 tablespoons finely chopped cilantro
1/4 cup orange juice
2 hard-cooked eggs, quartered, to garnish
Lime wedges, to garnish

Preheat oven to 350F (175C).

Wipe fish with damp paper towels. Rub lime juice into fish. Arrange fish in a shallow ovenproof dish. Season lightly with salt and pepper. Heat oil in a medium-size saucepan. Add onion, bell pepper, pumpkin seeds and half the cilantro. Cook until mixture is soft, but not brown, 5 to 10 minutes.

Spread mixture over fish. Pour orange juice over fish. Cover and bake 15 to 20 minutes or until fish turns from translucent to opaque. Garnish with egg quarters, lime wedges and remaining cilantro.

Makes 4 servings.

FISH IN SPICY TOMATO SAUCE

2 tablespoons butter
1 teaspoon hot chili powder
2 medium-size onions, finely chopped
1 garlic clove crushed in 1/4 teaspoon salt
2-1/2 cups chicken stock
2 tablespoons tomato paste
Juice of 1 lemon
2 teaspoons honey
1 pound cod or haddock fillet, cut in l-inch pieces
Salt and pepper
Steamed rice, to serve

Melt butter in a saucepan. Add chili powder and cook over low heat 1 minute. Add onions and garlic; cook 3 minutes. Stir in stock, tomato paste, lemon juice and honey. Cover and simmer 30 minutes or until quite thick.

Add fish and simmer 10 minutes. Season with salt and pepper. Serve over steamed rice.

Makes 4 servings.

Variation: Substitute 8 ounces peeled cooked shrimp for 8 ounces of fish; add shrimp after fish has cooked 5 minutes.

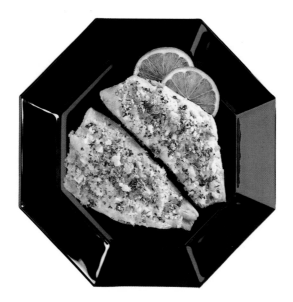

— RED SNAPPER IN CILANTRO —

2 pounds red snapper or other firm white fish fillets
1/4 cup fresh lime juice
Salt
1/4 cup olive oil
3/4 cup fresh white bread crumbs
1 garlic clove, finely chopped
6 tablespoons chopped cilantro
1 teaspoon grated lime peel
Pepper

Rinse fish with cold water and pat dry with paper towels. Lightly oil a heavy skillet. Rub fish with half the lime juice and 1 teaspoon salt and place into skillet, skin-side down.

Add enough cold water to almost cover fish. Bring to a boil, then reduce heat and simmer 5 minutes. In another pan, heat half the oil, then add bread crumbs, garlic and 4 tablespoons of the cilantro. Cook over low heat, stirring constantly, until crumbs are browned. Spread over fish. Simmer 5 minutes or until fish turns from translucent to opaque.

Mix the remaining lime juice and oil together and pour over fish. Cook 2 or 3 minutes. Combine remaining cilantro, lime peel and pepper and sprinkle over fish.

Makes 4 to 6 servings.

MEXICALI CHICKEN

2 tablespoons vegetable oil
1 medium-size onion, chopped
1 small green chile, seeded and chopped
1 garlic clove, finely chopped
2 tablespoons tomato paste
1 teaspoon ground cumin
1 tablespoon finely chopped cilantro
1 (8-oz.) can red kidney beans
1 pound tomatoes, peeled, chopped
1 pound cooked chicken, shredded
Salt and pepper
Steamed rice or warm tortillas and a green salad,
    to serve

Heat oil in a heavy saucepan over medium heat Add onion, chile and garlic; cook until onion is soft but not brown.

Stir in tomato paste, cumin, cilantro, beans, tomatoes and chicken; season with salt and pepper. Cover and simmer 20 minutes until thick; if necessary, uncover and simmer 10 minutes more. Serve with steamed rice or tortillas and a salad.

Makes 4 servings.

MOLE POBLANO

About 1/2 cup vegetable oil
1 (8-1b.) turkey, cut in serving portions
1 large onion, chopped
2 garlic cloves, finely chopped

Sauce:
6 ancho chiles, seeded and chopped
6 mulata chiles, seeded and chopped
4 pasilla chiles, seeded and chopped
1 cup slivered blanched almonds
1/3 cup roasted peanuts
1/4 cup sesame seeds
1/2 teaspoon coriander seeds
1/4 teaspoon anise seeds
2 whole cloves
1 (1/2-inch) piece cinnamon stick
2 medium-size onions, chopped
2 garlic cloves, finely chopped
1 pound tomatoes, peeled, seeded and chopped
1/3 cup raisins
2 Corn or Wheat Tortillas, page 13/14, cut in small
     pieces
1-1/2 ounces semisweet chocolate, chopped
Salt
Steamed rice; Basic Beans, page 15; and Christmas
     Salad, page 81; to serve

Heat 2 tablespoons of the oil in a large
heavy skillet, add turkey pieces, a few
at a time, and cook until browned all
over. Add more oil as necessary. Transfer
turkey to a large heavy flameproof casserole dish or saucepan. Add onion, garlic and enough water to cover. Simmer
1 hour or until turkey is tender. Using
a slotted spoon, remove turkey, cover
and keep warm. Strain and reserve stock.
Wash and dry casserole dish.

Meanwhile, soak chiles in a bowl with 2 cups warm water; let stand 30 minutes, stirring occasionally. To make sauce, in a blender or food processor fitted with the metal blade, process almonds, peanuts, half the sesame seeds, the coriander seeds, anise seeds, cloves and cinnamon. Transfer to a bowl.

In same blender or food processor, combine chiles and water, onions, garlic, tomatoes, raisins and tortillas; process to a thick paste, in batches if necessary. Transfer to a bowl and stir in ground nuts and spices. Measure oil left in skillet and add enough to make 1/4 cup. Put skillet over heat, add paste and fry, stirring, 5 minutes. Transfer to casserole dish. Stir in 2 cups reserved turkey stock and chocolate. Season with salt, simmer until chocolate has melted and sauce has the consistency of thick cream. Cover and simmer gently, stirring occasionally 20 minutes.

Add turkey pieces to sauce, turning them to coat well. Cover and simmer 10 minutes. Arrange turkey in a large, deep, warmed serving dish, and add sauce. In a small skillet over low heat, toast remaining sesame seeds and sprinkle over turkey. Serve with rice, beans and Christmas Salad.

Makes 10 servings.

CARNITAS

1 onion, chopped
3 garlic cloves
3 tablespoons vinegar
Salt and pepper
Pinch of sugar
1 (3-1b.) pork shoulder
2-1/2 cups water
1 cup lard, cut in pieces
Warm Tortillas, page 13/14, to serve

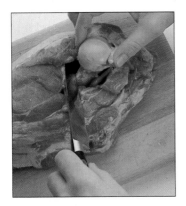

Put onion, garlic, vinegar, salt, pepper and sugar in a blender or food processor fitted with the metal blade; process until smooth. Transfer to a bowl.

Remove bone from meat; reserve bone. Cut meat in large chunks, add to onion mixture and stir to coat well. Put into a flameproof dish, cover and refrigerate overnight. Reheat oven to 325F (165C). Add water, reserved bone and lard to casserole dish. Cover and bake 2 hours, basting and turning occasionally.

Using a slotted spoon, lift out meat, and put into a roasting pan. Bake 30 minutes or until meat is golden brown. Meanwhile, skim all the fat from liquid in casserole dish; discard bone. Boil liquid rapidly until reduced to 1/3 cup. Transfer meat to a warmed serving dish and top with sauce. Serve with warm Tortillas.

Makes 6 servings.

—— MEXICAN PORK CHOPS ——

2 garlic cloves, halved
4 pork chops
2 tablespoons olive oil
1 medium-size avocado, to garnish
1 tablespoon lemon juice

Sauce:
3 green chiles, finely chopped
1-1/2 pounds tomatoes, peeled and chopped
2 small onions, chopped
1 garlic clove
Salt

Rub garlic over chops; cover and refrigerate 5 hours. To make sauce, put chiles into a saucepan, cover with water and bring to a boil; cook 3 minutes. Drain. Remove stems and cut chiles in half lengthwise. Discard white pith and seeds. Put chiles into a blender or food processor fitted with the metal blade, add tomatoes, onions, garlic and salt and process until pureed; set aside.

Heat oil in a skillet. Add chops; cook 5 minutes on each side or until brown. Add chile mixture and simmer, uncovered, 15 minutes. Peel avocado. Cut in half and remove seed. Slice and sprinkle with lemon juice. Put chops on a warmed serving plate, top with sauce and garnish with avocado slices.

Makes 4 servings.

EMPANADAS

Pastry:
1-1/2 cups self-rising flour
1/4 cup unsalted butter, diced, chilled
1/4 cup lard, diced, chilled
1 tablespoon lemon juice
About 1/3 cup cold water
Beaten egg, to glaze

Filling:
1/2 recipe Cooked Tomato Sauce, page 17
1/2 recipe Refried Beans, page 16
1 recipe Picadillo, page 18

For pastry, sift flour into a medium-size bowl. Toss in butter and lard. Carefully stir in lemon juice and enough water to make a soft dough. Place on a lightly floured surface. Using a floured rolling pin, roll out to a rectangle 1 inch thick. Lightly mark pastry crosswise in thirds. Fold up lowest third over dough; seal, fold top third down over dough. Seal edges with a rolling pin. Give pastry a quarter turn. Repeat rolling, folding and turning 3 times.

Put pastry in a plastic bag and refrigerate 1 hour. Meanwhile, prepare Cooked Tomato Sauce and Refried Beans.

Preheat oven to 425F (220C).

Lightly grease a baking sheet. On a lightly floured surface, using a floured rolling pin, roll out pastry to 1/8 inch thick. Cut out 8 (6-inch) circles. On one half of each circle put a spoonful of Picadillo, a spoonful of sauce, then a spoonful of Refried Beans.

Dampen edges with cold water. Fold pastry over filling; seal edges well, brush with egg and place on a baking sheet, spaced well apart.

Bake about 20 minutes or until golden brown and puffed. Serve hot or cold.

Makes 8 servings.

──── PORK COASTAL STYLE ────

2 tablespoons olive oil
1 (2-1b.) pork fillet, cut in (l-inch) cubes
3/4 cup all-purpose flour, seasoned with salt and
    pepper
1 large onion, chopped
2 cups beef stock
1 teaspoon ground coriander
1 garlic clove, finely chopped
1 green chile, seeded and chopped
2 tomatoes, peeled and chopped
1 red bell pepper, chopped
1/2 fresh pineapple, cut in chunks, or 1 (20-oz.)
    can pineapple chunks, drained
2 medium-size sweet potatoes, peeled and diced
1 tablespoon finely chopped cilantro, to garnish

Preheat oven to 350F (175C). Heat oil in a large heavy skillet. Toss pork in flour, add to skillet and cook until evenly browned, turning frequently. Transfer meat to a large flameproof casserole dish. Add onion to skillet and cook until soft; add a little more oil if necessary. Stir in stock and bring to a boil, stirring. Add coriander, garlic, chile, tomatoes and bell pepper. Simmer 5 minutes. Add to pork in dish.

Bring to a boil, cover and bake 1-1/2 to 2 hours or until tender. Add pineapple and sweet potatoes. Return to oven and bake 20 to 25 minutes or until potatoes are tender. Garnish with cilantro.

Makes 6 servings.

— CHICKEN ENCHILADAS —

1/4 cup olive oil
1 medium-size onion, finely chopped
1 garlic clove, finely chopped
4 green chiles, seeded and finely chopped
3 tomatoes, peeled and chopped
1 tablespoon finely chopped fresh cilantro
Salt
8 ounces cooked chicken, shredded
4 ounces queso fresco or Monterey Jack cheese,
    shredded (1 cup)
1-1/4 cups plain yogurt
12 Whole-Wheat Tortillas, page 14

Preheat oven to 350F (175C).

Grease a shallow ovenproof dish. In a heavy skillet, heat 1 tablespoon of the oil. Add onion and garlic; cook until golden brown, stirring frequently. Add chiles, tomatoes, cilantro and salt. Simmer 15 minutes or until thickened. Remove from heat and set aside. In a bowl, combine chicken, cheese and yogurt; set aside. Heat remaining oil in a skillet.

Using tongs, place one tortilla in oil 3 to 5 seconds or until softened. Repeat on other side, then drain on paper towels. Fill each tortilla with chicken mixture and roll up. Arrange seam-side down and close together in prepared dish. Pour tomato mixture over enchiladas and cover with foil. Bake 20 minutes or until heated through.

Makes 6 servings.

— MEATBALLS IN HOT SAUCE —

Meatballs:
2 pounds ground pork
1 large onion, finely chopped
2 garlic cloves, finely chopped
1/2 cup ground almonds
1 cup fresh bread crumbs
1 egg, lightly beaten
1 tablespoon finely chopped cilantro
3/4 teaspoon ground cinnamon
3 tablespoons dry sherry
Salt and pepper
2 tablespoons butter
2 tablespoons olive oil

Sauce:
1 tablespoon vegetable oil
1 large onion, finely chopped
1 garlic clove, crushed
1 teaspoon brown sugar
6 medium-size tomatoes, peeled and chopped
1 medium-size green bell pepper, sliced
1 medium-size red bell pepper, sliced
1 green chile, finely chopped
1/4 teaspoon red (cayenne) pepper
1 teaspoon paprika
1 tablespoon finely chopped cilantro
1/3 cup beef stock
2 teaspoons cornstarch
1/4 cup dry sherry
Salt and pepper

For meatballs, in a large bowl, mix together pork, onion, garlic, almonds, bread
crumbs, egg, cilantro, cinnamon, sherry,
salt and pepper. Using wet hands, form
mixture into 36 meatballs.

Melt butter and oil in a skillet. Add meatballs, a few at a time; cook 5 minutes or until well browned. Drain on paper towels. Keep warm.

To make sauce, put oil, onion, garlic and sugar into a saucepan. Cook over medium heat about 8 minutes. Add tomatoes, bell peppers, chile, cayenne, paprika and cilantro. Simmer 3 minutes. Add stock.

In a small bowl, mix cornstarch and sherry to a paste; stir into pan. Bring to a boil, stirring, then reduce heat and simmer 2 minutes; season with salt and pepper. Add meatballs and simmer 20 to 25 minutes or until sauce is fairly thick.

Makes 6 servings.

— RUM MARINATED STEAK —

2/3 cup rum
2 garlic cloves, crushed
1 teaspoon chili powder
1 tablespoon finely chopped cilantro
1/2 teaspoon hot pepper sauce
1 (2-1b.) beef sirloin steak, 2 inches thick
Mexicali Rice, page 94, Refried Beans, page 16,
    and a salad, to serve

Mix together rum, garlic, chile powder, cilantro and hot pepper sauce in a small bowl.

Wipe steak with damp paper towels. Place in a shallow dish and add rum mixture. Cover, and let stand at least 30 minutes, but preferably refrigerated overnight. Bring to room temperature before cooking, about 45 minutes. Remove steak from dish; reserve marinade. Preheat grill or broiler.

Grill steak 5 minutes on each side, or longer if desired, turning occasionally and basting frequently with marinade. Carve steak into thin slices. Serve with Mexicali Rice, Refried Beans, and a salad.

Makes 4 servings .

Note: If steak has been in refrigerator overnight, bring to room temperature 45 minutes before cooking.

— OVEN CHILE CON CARNE —

2 tablespoons olive oil
2 tablespoons all-purpose flour
Salt and pepper
1 pound beef stew meat, cut in 1-inch cubes
1 bay leaf
1 large onion, chopped
1 garlic clove, finely chopped
2 teaspoons hot chile powder
1 pound tomatoes, peeled and chopped
2 tablespoons tomato paste
1/4 recipe Basic Beans, page 15

Preheat oven to 325F (165C).

In a large skillet, heat oil. Season flour with salt and pepper. Toss meat in seasoned flour. Add to skillet; cook until evenly browned, stirring frequently. Add more oil if necessary to prevent sticking. Using a slotted spoon remove meat; drain on paper towels, then put into a casserole dish. Add bay leaf. Add onion and garlic to skillet; cook 5 minutes. Stir in chile powder, tomatoes and tomato paste.

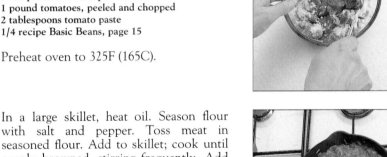

Pour over meat in casserole dish. Cover and bake 1 hour 20 minutes or until meat is tender. Remove from oven, and stir in beans. Cover, return to oven and cook 15 minutes or until heated through.

Makes 6 to 8 servings.

GRILLED STEAK

1 (1-1/4-1bs.) beef sirloin steak
2 tablespoons vegetable oil
1 tablespoon chopped cilantro
Salt and pepper
1/3 cup fresh orange juice
1 tablespoon fresh lime juice
2 teaspoons cider vinegar
Orange slices, to garnish

Wipe meat with damp paper towels. Put into a shallow dish. Combine oil, cilantro, salt, pepper, orange juice, lime juice and vinegar in a bowl. Pour over steak, cover and refrigerate overnight.

Bring to room temperature 45 minutes before cooking. Preheat grill or broiler. Lift steak from marinade allowing excess to drain off. Grill 5 minutes on each side, or longer if desired, basting with marinade. Cook for a little longer if well-cooked meat is preferred. Garnish with orange slices.

Makes 4 servings.

—— LAMB WITH RED WINE ——

3 green chiles, seeded and finely chopped
1-1/4 cups red wine
2 garlic cloves
2 thin slices gingerroot, peeled
1 teaspoon ground cumin
1 tablespoon finely chopped cilantro
Salt
8 small lamb loin chops, 2 pounds total weight

Put chiles, wine, garlic, gingerroot, cumin, cilantro and salt into a blender or food processor fitted with the metal blade, and process until pureed. Press through a sieve.

Wipe lamb with damp paper towels. Place in a large shallow ovenproof dish. Pour chile mixture over lamb, cover and place in refrigerator to marinate 8 hours, turning occasionally. Preheat oven to 350F (175C). Cover dish with foil and bake 1 hour or until chops are very tender.

Makes 4 servings.

—CHORIZO & CHEESE CREPES—

8 ounces chorizo, chopped
6 ounces Cheddar cheese, shredded (1-1/2 cups)

Crepes:
1 cup all-purpose flour, sifted
2 eggs
2/3 cup milk
5 tablespoons water
Salt
About 4 tablespoons melted butter, for cooking
    crepes

Tomato Sauce:
2 tablespoons olive oil
1 small onion, finely chopped
1 garlic clove, finely chopped
2 large tomatoes, peeled and chopped
3 tablespoons tomato paste
1 bay leaf
Salt and pepper
1 green chile, seeded and chopped
1/3 cup dairy sour cream
1 tablespoon finely chopped cilantro

To make crepes, put flour, eggs, milk, water and salt into a blender or food processor fitted with the metal blade. Process 1 minute at high speed. Scrape down sides of blender or processor with a spatula and blend again 15 seconds or until smooth.

Heat some of the butter in a 6-inch crepe pan or heavy skillet over medium heat. Pour in about 1/4 cup batter to thinly coat bottom. Quickly tilt pan in all directions to allow batter to coat the bottom evenly. Cook 1 minute, then, using a spatula, turn over crepe. Cook 30 to 60 seconds or until set and speckled brown. Slide onto a warmed plate and cover with a towel. Repeat until batter is used.

Preheat oven to 350F (175C). Grease a shallow ovenproof dish.

To make sauce, heat oil in a saucepan. Add onion and garlic; cook until soft. Add tomatoes, tomato paste, bay leaf, salt and pepper. Simmer 15 minutes. Discard bay leaf. Pour into a blender or food processor with chile and sour cream and process until smooth. Stir in cilantro.

Pour half the tomato sauce into dish. Divide chorizo and half the cheese evenly among crepes. Roll up tightly and place seam-side down in dish. Top with remaining sauce and sprinkle with remaining cheese. Bake 15 to 20 minutes or until bubbly.

Makes 6 servings.

──── HOT CHILE SAUCE ────

1 garlic clove
1 teaspoon chile powder
1 jalapeno, chopped
2 dried red chiles, chopped
1 green chile, chopped
1-1/4 cups water
2/3 cup dairy sour cream
Salt and pepper

Place all ingredients except salt and pepper in a blender or food processor fitted with the metal blade and process until smooth. Season. Transfer to a small serving bowl. Serve as a sauce.

Makes 2 cups.

Note: Keeps up to 24 hours in a covered container in the refrigerator.

SALSA FRESCA

4 large tomatoes, coarsely chopped
1 tablespoon finely chopped cilantro
1/2 small onion, finely chopped
2 green chiles, finely chopped
Juice of 1/2 lemon
1/2 teaspoon salt
1 teaspoon freshly ground pepper

Mix all ingredients together and let stand 15 minutes before serving. Serve as an accompaniment to any bean, rice or meat dish.

Makes 1-1/4 cups .

Note: Fresh salsa does not keep long, so if there is any left, cook it in a little olive oil and serve as a sauce for enchiladas , or over Ranch-Style Eggs, page 38, for breakfast.

GREEN CHILE RELISH

1 garlic clove crushed in 1/2 teaspoon salt
1 small onion, very finely chopped
6 green or red tomatoes, peeled, seeded and finely
   chopped
6 green chiles, seeded and very finely chopped
Salt and pepper
2 tablespoons olive oil
1 tablespoon white wine vinegar

In medium-size bowl, combine garlic, onion, tomatoes and chiles. In a small bowl, stir together salt, pepper, oil and vinegar.

Pour over tomato and chile mixture. Stir well. Transfer to a serving bowl.

Makes 2/3 cup.

Note: Keeps up to 24 hours in a covered container in the refrigerator.

ALMOND SAUCE

2 tablespoons vegetable oil
1/2 small onion, very finely chopped
1 small garlic clove, chopped
2 tablespoons sugar
2 tablespoons vinegar
3 tablespoons tomato paste
1/2 cup ground almonds (2 ounces)
Salt and pepper

Heat oil in a medium-size saucepan. Add onion and garlic; cook, stirring occasionally until soft but not brown. Add sugar, vinegar, tomato paste and ground almonds.

Bring slowly to a boil, stirring constantly, then reduce heat and simmer 2 minutes. Season with salt and pepper. Serve hot with fish or chicken.

Makes 4 servings.

SALSA VERDE

1 pound tomatillos, peeled and coarsely chopped
1/2 onion, finely chopped
1 tablespoon finely chopped cilantro
Salt and pepper

Put all ingredients into a bowl and mix together well. For a smoother consistency, put all the ingredients in a blender or food processor fitted with the metal blade: process until finely chopped.

Use as a sauce for tacos or as an accompaniment to a meal.

Makes 2 cups.

SALAD DRESSING

3 tablespoons vegetable oil
1 tablespoon vinegar
1/4 teaspoon Dijon-style mustard
Salt and pepper
1 tablespoon finely chopped cilantro

Put all the ingredients in a jar with a tight-fitting lid. Shake until blended. Store, in jar, in the refrigerator up to 3 days. Shake well before serving.

Makes 1/4 cup.

CHAYOTE SALAD

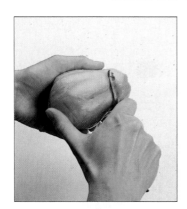

2 pounds chayotes
1/3 cup olive oil
2 teaspoons finely chopped cilantro
2 tablespoons white wine vinegar
Salt and pepper
1 avocado
3-1/2 ounces mozzarella cheese, cut in strips
8 pitted green olives, sliced

Peel chayotes, halve, discard seeds and chop. Steam over boiling, salted water about 20 minutes or until tender. Cool. In a jar with a tight-fitting lid, shake together olive oil, cilantro, vinegar, salt and pepper.

Cut avocado in half lengthwise, discard seed and slice into a serving bowl. Immediately toss with the olive oil dressing. Toss in chayotes, cheese and olives.

Makes 4 servings.

CHRISTMAS SALAD

1 head romaine lettuce
2 small cooked beets, sliced
1 apple
1 large carrot, finely diced
1/4 fresh pineapple, diced, or 1 (14-oz.) can
    pineapple chunks, drained
1 banana
Fresh lemon juice
1/2 cup toasted slivered almonds, to garnish
1 orange, peeled, sectioned and chopped, to
    garnish

Dressing:
1 tablespoon lemon juice
3 tablespoons vegetable oil
Salt and pepper

Use half the lettuce leaves to line bottom
and sides of a shallow serving dish.
Arrange beets on lettuce around edge of
plate. Peel, core and slice apple. Arrange
apple slices over beets. Shred remaining lettuce and put into another bowl.
Add carrot and pineapple. Slice banana,
sprinkle with lemon juice and add to
bowl.

To make dressing, combine lemon juice,
oil, salt and pepper in a jar with a tight-
fitting lid; shake well. Pour over shredded
lettuce mixture. Toss gently. Pile salad in
center of plate. Garnish with almonds and
orange.

Makes 6 servings.

TOMATO SALAD

1 large avocado
1 teaspoon olive oil
1 teaspoon lemon juice
1 ounce cooked ham, diced
Salt and pepper
4 large lettuce leaves
4 medium-size tomatoes, thinly sliced
4 cilantro sprigs, to garnish

Cut avocado in half, remove seed and scoop flesh into a bowl. Add oil, lemon juice, ham, salt and pepper; mix well.

Line a serving dish with lettuce leaves. Arrange tomatoes on top, followed by avocado mixture. Garnish with cilantro.

Makes 4 servings.

—— GREEN ONION SALAD ——

8 green onions, cut in 1/2-inch slices
4 ounces zucchini, cut in l-inch slices
1 large green bell pepper, cut in strips
3 medium-size tomatoes, peeled, seeded and
    chopped
3 tablespoons olive oil
1 tablespoon white wine vinegar
Salt and black pepper
1 tablespoon chopped cilantro, to garnish

Boil green onions in salted water 3 minutes or until crisp-tender. Drain. Put into a serving bowl. Boil zucchini in salted water 5 minutes or until crisp-tender. Drain. Add to onions with bell pepper and tomatoes.

Put oil, vinegar, salt and black pepper into a jar with a tight-fitting lid. Shake well and pour over vegetables. Toss gently, then cover and refrigerate until chilled. Toss again just before serving, and garnish with cilantro.

Makes 4 servings.

TACOS

12 Corn Tortillas, page 13
Vegetable oil, for deep-frying

Filling:
1/2 head iceberg lettuce, shredded
1 recipe Picadillo, page 18
1 large onion, finely chopped
6 large tomatoes, peeled, finely chopped

Heat oil in a deep-fat fryer to 350F (175C).

Fry tortillas by holding two at a time with tongs, and pressing them against side of pot to make a U-shape. Hold in position about 1 minute, then separate two tortillas and fry about 3 minutes or until golden brown. They should hold their shape, but if they do not, hold a little longer with tongs. Drain on paper towels.

Put a layer of lettuce in each taco shell. Spoon Picadillo onto lettuce, then top with onion, tomatoes and another layer of lettuce to finish. Serve immediately.

Makes 6 servings.

Variation: Top lettuce with shredded cooked chicken; a layer of Guacamole, page 26; and a spoonful of sour cream. Garnish with pickled jalapenos.

MEXICAN SALAD

8 ounces small new potatoes
2 large carrots, diced
1 turnip, diced
1/2 small cauliflower, divided into flowerets
3 small gherkins
1 tablespoon capers
6 pitted ripe olives
1/4 cup mayonnaise
1 teaspoon Dijon-style mustard

Dressing:
1/3 cup olive oil
2 tablespoons wine vinegar
Salt and pepper

Boil potatoes in lightly salted water about 10 minutes or until tender. Drain and set aside. Boil carrots and turnip in lightly salted water 8 to 10 minutes or until tender. Drain and set aside. Cook cauliflower in lightly salted boiling water 5 minutes or until crisp-tender. Drain. While still warm, mix together all the vegetables in a bowl.

To make dressing, combine oil, vinegar, salt and pepper in a jar with a tight-fitting lid and shake well. Pour over the vegetables and toss gently. Put gherkins in center of a serving plate. Arrange capers and olives around gherkins. Arrange vegetables around outside of plate. Put mayonnaise and mustard into a small bowl and mix well. Drizzle mayonnaise mixture over vegetables. Serve at room temperature.

Makes 4 to 6 servings.

─── VEGETABLE SALAD ───

1 pound zucchini, cut in 1/2-inch slices
1 (10-oz.) package thawed frozen green peas
1 celery stalk, sliced
1 tablespoon chili powder
1 small garlic clove, chopped
1/4 teaspoon ground cumin
1 teaspoon fresh thyme or 1/2 teaspoon dried leaf
    thyme
1/4 cup water
1/4 cup red wine vinegar
1 bay leaf
Salt and pepper
1/4 cup olive oil

In a large bowl, mix zucchini, peas and celery. Put chili powder, garlic, cumin and thyme into a small bowl and mash to a paste. Carefully stir into vegetables. Put water and vinegar in a small saucepan and bring to a boil. Pour over vegetables and stir in bay leaf, salt and pepper. Cover bowl and refrigerate 48 hours. Two hours before serving, stir in oil.

Remove bay leaf. Adjust seasoning and serve as an accompaniment to meat and bean dishes.

Makes 4 servings

— POTATOES VINAIGRETTE —

1 pound potatoes, sliced
1 tablespoon finely chopped cilantro
1 tablespoon olive oil
2 tablespoons malt vinegar
Salt and pepper
2 green onions, coarsely chopped
8 pitted ripe olives, halved

Steam potatoes over boiling salted water 7 to 10 minutes or until tender. Put into a serving bowl. Add cilantro.

In a jar with a tight-fitting lid, shake together oil, vinegar, salt and pepper. Pour over potatoes and toss to combine. Sprinkle onions and olives over salad.

Makes 4 to 6 servings.

AVOCADO & CAULIFLOWER SALAD

1 small cauliflower, divided into flowerets
2 tablespoons white wine vinegar
Salt and pepper
4 small avocados
1/2 cup ground almonds (2 ounces)
1/2 teaspoon ground nutmeg
6 radishes, thinly sliced, to garnish

Cook cauliflower in boiling salted water for 5 minutes. Drain and cool, then put into a large bowl. Sprinkle with vinegar, salt and pepper and set aside.

Cut avocados in half, remove seeds and scoop flesh into a bowl and mash. Stir in almonds, nutmeg, salt and pepper. Mix well. Carefully combine with cauliflower and serve immediately. Serve garnished with radishes.

Makes 4 servings.

FRIED CORN

2 tablespoons olive oil
1 small onion, finely chopped
1/2 small green bell pepper, cut in thin rings
1/2 small red bell pepper, cut in thin rings
2 tablespoons chopped cilantro
1 green chile, seeded and finely chopped
1-3/4 cups whole-kernel corn
4 ounces button mushrooms
Salt and black pepper
8 cilantro sprigs, to garnish

Heat oil in a heavy skillet over medium heat. Add onion, bell peppers, chopped cilantro and chile. Cook 5 minutes, stirring occasionally or until soft. Stir in corn, mushrooms, salt and black pepper. Cook 5 minutes, stirring occasionally.

Transfer to a warmed serving dish and garnish with cilantro.

Makes 6 servings.

—— STUFFED BELL PEPPERS ——

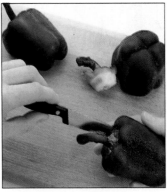

6 medium-size green peppers
2 tablespoons butter
1 medium-size onion, finely chopped
2 garlic cloves, finely chopped
1 pound lean ground pork
1 medium-size apple
2 peaches
1/2 cup raisins
1/2 cup walnuts, finely chopped
3 tablespoons finely chopped cilantro
1 teaspoon ground cinnamon
1/2 teaspoon ground cloves
Salt and black pepper
2 tablespoons sugar
1/4 cup dry sherry
1-1/4 cups hot water
Corn Tortillas, page 13, or Mexican Rice, page 94, to serve

Sauce:
2 (3-oz.) packages cream cheese
2/3 cup dairy sour cream
1/2 cup walnuts, finely chopped
1 garlic clove, crushed
1/4 teaspoon ground cumin

Preheat broiler. Put bell peppers on a baking sheet and broil about 3 inches from heat, turning so they char evenly. When cool enough to handle, peel off all skin. Discard stems, white membrane and seeds; set peppers aside.

Melt butter in a skillet. Add onion and garlic; cook until soft. Add pork, and cook 5 minutes, stirring constantly. Peel, core and chop apple; seed and chop peaches. Stir apple, peaches, raisins, walnuts, 1 tablespoon cilantro, cinnamon, cloves, salt, black pepper, sugar, sherry and hot water into skillet. Simmer 10 minutes or until liquid has evaporated. Remove from heat, cover and keep hot.

To make sauce, in a bowl, stir together cream cheese, sour cream, walnuts, garlic and cumin. Season with salt.

Fill peeled peppers with pork mixture, spoon sauce over the top, and garnish with remaining cilantro. Serve immediately with Tortillas or Mexican Rice.

Makes 6 servings.

— CARROTS WITH TEQUILA —

1 pound carrots
1/4 cup butter
1/4 teaspoon dried dill weed, crushed
Salt and pepper
1/4 cup tequila

Cut carrots diagonally in 1/4-inch-thick slices. Melt butter in a skillet over low heat. Add carrots. Increase heat to medium and cook carrots 10 minutes, stirring occasionally. Add dill weed, salt and pepper. Mix well. Increase heat to high.

Pour tequila over carrots, then ignite using a long match. When flames have died down, stir and serve immediately.

Makes 4 servings.

VEGETABLE-FILLED ENCHILADAS

1/4 cup vegetable oil
1 large onion, chopped
1 garlic clove
1 green chile, finely chopped
2 red bell peppers, seeded and chopped
4 large tomatoes, peeled and chopped
1 bay leaf
2 tablespoons chopped cilantro
1 cup beef stock
1/2 cup dairy sour cream
Salt
12 Whole-Wheat Tortillas, page 14
1/2 recipe Cooked Tomato Sauce, page 17
2 ounces Cheddar cheese, shredded (1/2 cup)

Heat half the oil in a heavy skillet. Add onion, garlic and chile; cook until soft. Add bell peppers; cook until crisp-tender. Add tomatoes, bay leaf, cilantro and stock, cook 1 or 2 minutes. Remove from heat and stir in sour cream and salt. Discard bay leaf. Divide tomato mixture among the tortillas, spooning mixture in center of tortillas.

Fold over tortilla edges, sides to middle; then fold the ends under to enclose completely. Secure with wooden picks. In a saucepan, gently heat tomato sauce, stirring occasionally and keep warm. Meanwhile, heat remaining oil in a heavy skillet. Add tortilla bundles, sealed-side down, cook 2 minutes on each side until golden. Transfer to a warmed serving dish. Top with tomato sauce and sprinkle with cheese.

Makes 6 servings.

MEXICAN RICE

1-1/2 cups long-grain rice
2 tablespoons vegetable oil
1 large onion, chopped
2 garlic cloves, finely chopped
4 to 6 fresh hot red or green chiles
2 medium-size tomatoes, peeled, seeded and
    chopped
4 cups chicken stock
Salt and pepper
1/3 cup cooked or thawed frozen green peas
Cilantro sprigs, to garnish

Put rice into a bowl, cover with boiling water and let stand 30 minutes. Drain. Pour into a strainer and let stand 1 hour to dry. Heat oil in a heavy skillet over low heat. Stir in rice until all grains are well coated with oil. Add onion, garlic and chiles. Cook until onion is transparent and rice is golden. Add tomatoes and stock; season with salt and pepper. Cover and simmer 20 to 30 minutes or until liquid has been absorbed and rice is tender and fluffy; add peas 5 minutes before end of cooking.

If a softer rice is preferred, stir in a little more stock after 20 minutes and continue cooking until additional liquid has been absorbed. Transfer to a warmed serving dish and garnish with cilantro.

Makes 6 to 8 servings.

—— KIDNEY BEAN STEW ——

1 onion, halved
1 tablespoon olive oil
1 tablespoon finely chopped cilantro
1 chile, seeded and finely chopped
1 small tomato, peeled and finely chopped
1/2 recipe Basic Beans, page 15
Salt
2 ounces Cheddar cheese, shredded (1/2 cup), to
  garnish

Finely chop half the onion. Heat oil in a saucepan. Add chopped onion and cook until soft but not brown. Add cilantro, chile and tomato. Cook 5 minutes. Stir in beans and season with salt. Heat through. Slice the remaining onion half.

Transfer beans to individual warmed bowls. Garnish with onion slices and cheese.

Makes 4 servings.

GREEN RICE

1 large green bell pepper, coarsely chopped
1 small onion, coarsely chopped
2 garlic cloves
1/4 cup chopped cilantro
3 tablespoons olive oil
1 cup long-grain rice
2-1/2 cups chicken stock
Salt and black pepper

Put bell pepper, onion, garlic and cilantro into a blender or food processor fitted with the metal blade and process until finely chopped. Heat 1 tablespoon of the oil in a small saucepan. Stir in onion mixture and cook, stirring, 3 minutes. Heat remaining oil in a heavy skillet. Add rice. Stir over medium heat until light brown.

Add onion mixture, stock, salt and black pepper. Bring to a boil. Reduce heat, cover and simmer 10 minutes or until liquid is absorbed. Reduce heat to very low and steam, still covered, 30 to 40 minutes until rice is tender. Add more stock if necessary to keep rice moist. Adjust seasoning. Transfer to a warm serving dish.

Makes 4 to 6 servings.

—— SPINACH WITH PIMENTO ——

2 pounds fresh spinach
1/4 cup olive oil
1 garlic clove, crushed
2 tablespoons butter
2 tablespoons all-purpose flour
2/3 cup milk
Salt and black pepper
2 hard-cooked eggs, sliced, to garnish
2 large red bell peppers, cut in strips, to garnish

Rinse spinach thoroughly and shake off excess water. Heat oil in a large saucepan. Add garlic and stir 1 minute. Add spinach and cook over medium heat, stirring constantly or until tender. Drain and chop.

Heat butter in pan, stir in flour and cook 2 minutes, stirring constantly. Gradually stir in milk until mixture is very thick. Cook 2 minutes, stirring constantly. Add spinach and heat through. Season to taste. Transfer to warm serving dish. Garnish with eggs and bell peppers.

Makes 4 servings.

—ORANGE BREAD PUDDING—

10 slices day-old bread, crusts removed, cubed
1 (12-oz.) can mandarin oranges, drained
1/3 cup raisins
1/2 cup chopped almonds
1/4 cup butter, diced
2-1/2 cups milk
3 eggs
2/3 cup packed dark brown sugar
1/2 teaspoon freshly grated nutmeg
1/2 teaspoon ground cinnamon
1 teaspoon vanilla extract

Preheat oven to 350F (175C). Grease a 13-inch x 9-inch baking pan. Mix together bread, oranges, raisins and almonds. Transfer to prepared baking pan.

In a saucepan over low heat, heat butter and milk to just below the simmering point, but do not boil. Remove from heat.

In a large bowl, stir together eggs, sugar, spices and vanilla. Stir in milk and butter, then slowly pour mixture over bread mixture. Let stand 10 minutes for bread to absorb liquid. Bake 45 minutes or until set in center and golden brown and crisp on top.

Makes 6 servings.

—— CARAMEL CUSTARD ——

1 cup sugar
3-3/4 cups milk
Salt
1 teaspoon vanilla extract
3 eggs
6 egg yolks

Preheat oven to 300F (150C). Put half of the sugar into a heavy saucepan, place over a low heat and stir gently until sugar has melted. Cook without stirring until golden.

Pour into 6 individual ramekin dishes or custard dishes, turning them to coat the bottom and 1/2 inch up the side. Heat milk in a heavy saucepan over low heat. Add remaining sugar, salt and vanilla. Heat, stirring frequently or until sugar has dissolved, about 3 minutes. Beat eggs and egg yolks together in a bowl, then stir in hot milk. Strain through a sieve into caramel-lined dishes. Place in a baking pan and pour boiling water around dishes. Cover them with buttered waxed paper.

Bake 45 minutes or until a knife inserted off-center comes out clean. Remove dishes from pan and cool, then chill. To serve, dip bottom of dishes in hot water, then let stand for a few minutes. Shake gently to loosen and turn onto individual serving plates.

Makes 6 servings.

— CINNAMON ORANGES —

3 oranges, peeled and thinly sliced crosswise
1/4 cup sugar
1/4 teaspoon ground cinnamon

Place sliced oranges in a serving bowl. Mix sugar and cinnamon together in a small bowl; sprinkle over oranges.

Cover bowl and refrigerate at least 1 hour.

Makes 4 servings.

— LEMON-TEQUILA SOUFFLE —

3 lemons
3 eggs, separated
1/3 cup sugar
3 tablespoons tequila
4 teaspoons unflavored gelatin powder
2/3 cup whipping cream

Decoration:
2/3 cup whipping cream
Fresh mint leaves

Tie a 2-inch band of waxed paper around a 6-inch souffle dish. Brush dish and paper with oil. Grate peel from all lemons; squeeze juice from 2.

In a bowl, placed over a saucepan of hot water, whisk egg yolks, sugar and lemon peel until thick. Put tequila into a small bowl, sprinkle gelatin over the top and let stand 5 minutes to soften. Place bowl over a saucepan of hot water and stir until gelatin has dissolved. Remove bowl from pan; allow gelatin to cool slightly, stir in lemon juice, then stir slowly into lemon mixture.

Whisk cream until soft peaks form, then gently fold into lemon mixture until just evenly mixed. Set aside until nearly set. Whisk egg whites until stiff but not dry, then fold carefully into lemon mixture. Spoon into prepared dish. Refrigerate until set. To decorate, whip cream, spoon into a pastry bag fitted with a star tip. Pipe cream on top of souffle and decorate with mint leaves.

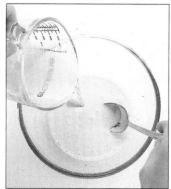

Makes 6 servings.

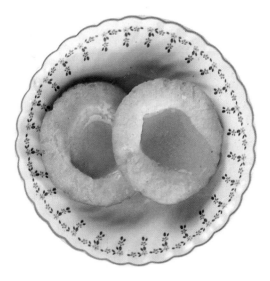

HONEYED FRITTERS

2 cups all-purpose flour
1/2 teaspoon baking powder
Salt
2 tablespoons sugar
1 egg, beaten
2 tablespoons butter, melted
About 1 cup milk
Vegetable oil for deep-frying

Syrup:
2 tablespoons honey
1 tablespoon rum
1 (3-inch) cinnamon stick or 1/2 teaspoon ground
    cinnamon
1 tablespoon butter

Sift flour, baking powder and salt into a large bowl. Stir in sugar, then add egg, butter and just enough milk to form a soft but not sticky dough. Turn onto a lightly floured surface and knead lightly until smooth. Divide dough in 8 to 12 pieces; shape each piece into a ball. Cover and let stand 30 minutes. On a lightly floured surface, shape balls into flat cakes. Using the back of a metal spoon, make a shallow indentation in the top of each cake. Heat a deep-fat fryer two-thirds full of oil to 375F (19OC). Fry a few cakes at a time 5 minutes or until golden brown and puffy. Drain on paper towels.

To make the syrup, place all ingredients in a heavy saucepan. Bring slowly to a boil, stirring frequently. Simmer, stirring occasionally, 20 minutes, or until mixture thickens to a syrup. Remove cinnamon stick. Serve fritters in individual bowls topped with syrup.

Makes 6 servings.

— MANGOES WITH CREAM —

1 cup water
1/2 cup sugar
1 (1/2-inch) cinnamon stick
3 mangoes, peeled and thickly sliced lengthwise
1 teaspoon vanilla extract
2/3 cup whipping cream
1/4 cup rum

Put water, half the sugar and cinnamon stick into a heavy saucepan. Bring to a boil, then reduce heat and simmer 20 to 30 minutes, stirring occasionally or until syrup thickens.   Add mango slices to syrup and simmer 5 to 10 minutes or until barely tender. Remove cinnamon stick and add vanilla. Transfer to a serving dish and cool.

Cover and refrigerate until chilled. Whip together cream and remaining sugar until soft peaks form. Fold in rum. Serve in a separate bowl to accompany mangoes.

Makes 6 servings.

— CHERRY CHIMICHANGAS —

2 tablespoons arrowroot
1-1/4 cups water
1/4 cup granulated sugar
8 ounces red tart cherries, pitted
Grated peel of 1 orange
8 Whole-Wheat Tortillas, page 14
1/3 cup butter or margarine
1/2 cup powdered sugar
1/2 cup (2 ounces) toasted slivered almonds, to
   decorate

In a saucepan, mix arrowroot with a little of the water to a smooth paste. Gradually stir in the remaining water, then granulated sugar. Bring to a boil over medium heat, stirring. Reduce heat and simmer 2 minutes. Remove from heat and stir in cherries and orange peel. Divide cherry mixture among tortillas. Fold each tortilla in half, then in half again.

Heat butter in a skillet. Add two filled tortillas and cook about 3 minutes on each side until golden brown. Transfer to a warmed serving plate and keep warm. Repeat with remaining tortillas, adding more butter if necessary. Sift powdered sugar over chimichangas and decorate with toasted almonds.

Makes 8 chimichangas.

PUMPKIN IN SYRUP

2 pounds pumpkin, weighed with skin and seeds
1 lemon
1-1/4 cups water
1/4 cup sugar
1 orange
1 tablespoon orange-flavored liqueur

Peel pumpkin and discard seeds. Cut flesh into bite-size pieces. Squeeze juice from lemon; reserve peel. Put the water, sugar and lemon juice into a large saucepan. Bring to a boil, stirring constantly.

Peel orange and reserve flesh. Remove all white pith from orange peel and lemon peel; cut in strips. Add peel to syrup. Add pumpkin. Simmer 10 minutes or until pumpkin is tender. Divide orange in sections, then chop into small pieces. Put into a serving bowl. Using a slotted spoon, remove pumpkin from syrup, and mix with orange in bowl. Remove citrus peels from syrup, and shred; reserve for decoration.

Boil remaining syrup until reduced to 2 tablespoons. Remove from heat and stir in liqueur. Add to pumpkin mixture. Cool to room temperature, then cover and refrigerate until chilled. Decorate with shredded peel.

Makes 6 servings .

— CARAMEL-RUM APPLES —

3/4 cup butter or margarine, in pieces
1/2 cup packed light brown sugar
2 teaspoons lemon juice
3 tablespoons water
6 medium-size apples
2 tablespoons rum
1/2 teaspoon ground cinnamon
Ice cream or whipped cream, to serve

Melt butter in a large saucepan over low heat. Stir in sugar, lemon juice and water. Simmer, stirring occasionally or until sugar has dissolved; then simmer without stirring until slightly thickened and golden, about 12 minutes.

Peel apples; using an apple corer, remove cores, then slice apples in rings. Add rum, cinnamon and apples to syrup, making sure apples are thoroughly coated with syrup. Simmer until apples are soft, about 5 minutes. Transfer to a serving dish. Serve warm with ice cream or cream.

Makes 4 to 6 servings.

CHOCOLATE & ORANGE MOUSSE

12 ounces semisweet chocolate, broken
1/4 cup water
1 tablespoon butter
1 tablespoon orange-flavored liqueur
4 eggs, separated
2/3 cup whipping cream, whipped, to decorate

Put chocolate in a bowl with water. Place bowl over a pan of simmering water until chocolate melts, stirring occasionally. Remove pan from heat and stir chocolate 5 minutes. Remove bowl from pan and stir butter and liqueur into chocolate.

In another bowl, whisk egg whites until stiff. Beat yolks into slightly cooled chocolate mixture, then gently fold in whites until just evenly mixed. Spoon mousse into individual glasses and refrigerate until set, about 1 hour. Decorate with whipped cream.

Makes 6 servings.

Note: Use fresh eggs without cracks.

ALMOND JELLY

1/4 cup water
1-1/2 tablespoons unflavored gelatin
1 cup boiling water
1 cup granulated sugar
1/4 teaspoon almond extract
6 egg whites
1 cup (5 ounces) blanched almonds

Custard:
4 cups milk
6 egg yolks
1/4 cup sugar
1 teaspoon vanilla extract
1/3 cup whipping cream

Rinse inside of a 5-cup mold with cold water. Turn upside down to drain well. Put the 1/4 cup water into a small bowl, sprinkle with gelatin and let stand 5 minutes to soften. Stir in boiling water until the gelatin has dissolved. Stir in sugar to dissolve; add almond extract. Refrigerate until beginning to thicken, about 10 minutes; beat until frothy.

In a large bowl, whisk egg whites until stiff but not dry. Gently fold into gelatin mixture. Pour half into prepared mold. Reserve some almonds for decoration; sprinkle remaining almonds over mixture. Top with remaining gelatin mixture. Refrigerate at least 4 hours, preferably overnight.

Make custard 45 minutes before serving. Heat milk to just below simmering. Meanwhile, in a bowl placed over a saucepan of hot water, whisk egg yolks with sugar until thick. Strain milk into yolks, stirring so mixture remains smooth.

Cook, stirring constantly with a wooden spoon until lightly thickened. Stir in vanilla, remove from heat and cool 10 minutes.

Whip cream until stiff. Fold into Custard; refrigerate 30 minutes. Unmold jelly on a serving plate, sprinkle with reserved almonds and serve with Custard.

Makes 8 servings.

Note: Use fresh eggs without cracks.

COMPOTE

1-1/3 cups (6 ounces) dried apricots
2/3 cup (4 ounces) pitted prunes
2/3 cup (4 ounces) dried peaches or pears,
    chopped
2/3 cup raisins
1/2 cup (2 ounces) blanched almonds
1 (2-inch) cinnamon stick
4 whole cloves
1/3 cup walnut halves, toasted, see Note

Put dried fruits, almonds, cinnamon and cloves into a saucepan; cover with water. Cover pan and simmer 15 minutes or until fruits are tender but not mushy. Remove from heat and cool to lukewarm. Remove cinnamon and cloves.

Spoon into individual glasses or serving bowl. Cover and refrigerate until chilled. Sprinkle with walnuts.

Makes 6 servings.

Note: To toast walnuts, spread on a baking sheet and place in a preheated 325F (165C) oven 15 minutes, turning frequently; watch closely to prevent burning.

— PECAN & ALMOND COOKIES —

2 eggs, separated
1/2 cup granulated sugar
1 teaspoon vanilla extract
3/4 cup all-purpose flour
1 teaspoon baking powder
1/4 cup mixed pecans and almonds, chopped
2 tablespoons powdered sugar
Mexican Hot Chocolate, page 115, to serve

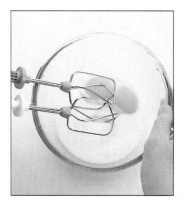

Preheat oven to 300F (150C). Grease 12 individual muffin cups. Whisk egg yolks with granulated sugar until thick and pale. Stir in vanilla. Sift together flour and baking powder over the surface of egg yolk mixture, then fold in.

In a clean bowl, whisk egg whites until stiff but not dry; fold gently into egg yolk mixture. Carefully fold in nuts. Divide between prepared cups and bake 15 minutes. Sift powdered sugar over cookies and serve warm with Mexican Hot Chocolate.

Makes 12

CINNAMON COOKIES

1 cup margarine, softened
1/2 cup sugar
1 teaspoon vanilla extract
3 cups all-purpose flour
2 teaspoons ground cinnamon
1-1/2 cups powdered sugar

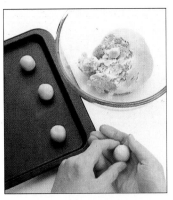

Grease 2 baking sheets. Beat together margarine, sugar and vanilla. Stir in flour and 1 teaspoon of the cinnamon to make a soft dough. Cover and refrigerate 1 hour.

Preheat oven to 350F (175C).

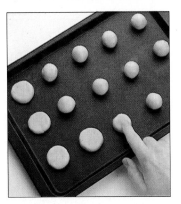

Form mixture in 1-inch balls and place on prepared baking sheets, leaving space between cookies. Bake 15 minutes or until lightly browned on bottom. Remove from oven, cool on baking sheets for a few minutes, then transfer to a wire rack to cool. Mix together powdered sugar and remaining cinnamon; sift over cookies.

Makes 24 cookies.

-APRICOT & COCONUT BALLS-

1-1/3 cups (6 ounces) dried apricots, finely
    chopped
2-1/2 cups (4 ounces) flaked coconut
1/2 cup (2 ounces) blanched almonds, finely
    chopped
1 teaspoon vanilla extract
1 (14-oz.) can sweetened condensed milk
Powdered sugar, sifted

Put apricots, coconut, almonds and vanilla
into a bowl; mix together. Stir in enough
condensed milk to make a stiff mixture.

Shape in l-inch balls. Roll in powdered
sugar, and place in small paper cups.

Makes 24.

PECAN CANDY

1-1/2 cups packed dark brown sugar
2/3 cup milk
3 tablespoons maple syrup
Salt
1-1/4 cups pecan halves
2 tablespoons butter, softened
1 teaspoon vanilla extract

Line a baking sheet with waxed paper. Put sugar, milk, maple syrup and salt into a large heavy saucepan. Stir with a wooden spoon over medium heat until sugar has dissolved, then bring to a boil. Add nuts. Cook to the soft ball stage, 238F (115C). Remove from heat. Cool until lukewarm. Stir in butter and vanilla and beat about 2 minutes until mixture begins to thicken and becomes creamy.

Drop teaspoonfuls of mixture onto waxed paper. Let set. Store in a plastic bag in refrigerator up to 3 days.

Makes 18.

Note: To test for soft ball stage without a candy thermometer, drop a small amount of syrup into very cold water, you should be able to form a soft ball that will flatten.

— MEXICAN HOT CHOCOLATE —

8 ounces semisweet chocolate, chopped
3-3/4 cups milk, heated until hot
1/4 teaspoon ground cinnamon
1 teaspoon vanilla extract

Put chocolate in a large bowl and place over a saucepan of hot water until melted. Whisk in hot milk, then pour into a saucepan. Add cinnamon and vanilla. Bring almost to a boil. Reduce heat and whisk 2 minutes.

Remove from heat and whisk until bubbles form on top of liquid. Serve hot in individual cups, dividing foam equally, or leave until cold; whisk again before serving.

Makes 4 servings.

CAFE DE OLLA

5 cups water
1 (l-inch) piece cinnamon stick
2 whole cloves
1/4 cup packed brown sugar
1/4 cup freshly ground coffee

Put water, cinnamon and cloves into a saucepan, and bring to a boil. Reduce heat, add sugar and stir until dissolved. Stir in coffee and simmer 2 minutes.

Turn off heat and let stand, covered, about 5 minutes or until all coffee has settled. Strain into individual mugs.

Makes 4 servings.

MARGARITA

1 lime, halved
Salt
Crushed ice
1/4 cup tequila
1 tablespoon orange-flavored liqueur
Wedge of lime, to serve

Rub rim of a chilled cocktail glass with one of lime halves, then dip rim into salt. Add crushed ice to a cocktail shaker. Squeeze juice from remaining lime half.

Add lime juice, tequila and liqueur to shaker. Shake or stir well. Strain into glass. Serve with a wedge of lime to squeeze into drink.

Makes 1 serving.

—— TEQUILA SUNRISE ——

1/4 cup tequila
2/3 cup orange juice
1 tablespoon grenadine
1 teaspoon fresh lime juice
Crushed ice
Maraschino cherry, to decorate

Pour tequila, orange juice, grenadine and lime juice into a blender; mix well. Spoon crushed ice into a chilled tall glass.

Strain tequila mixture over ice. Decorate with a maraschino cherry on a wooden pick.

Makes 1 serving.

LIMONADE

1 lemon, quartered
2/3 cup sugar
4 cups cold water
Ice cubes
Mint sprigs, to decorate

Put lemon, sugar and 1-1/2 cups of the water into a blender; blend 40 seconds. Strain into a pitcher.

Pour the remaining water through strainer into pitcher. Chill well. Serve over ice cubes and decorate with mint.

Makes 6 servings.

INDEX